Buddhism
in Daily Life

By Nina van Gorkom

1996
New Edition

Triple Gem Press

Originally published (1969) in Thailand by The Dhamma Study and Propagation Foundation (no ISBN). First (revised) edition published in the UK by Triple Gem Press 1992 (ISBN 1 897633 05 2). Second (revised) edition published in 1996 by:

Triple Gem Press
46 Fircroft Road
Tooting Bec
London
SW17 7PS

ISBN 1 897633 16 5

Front cover: Oxford Street, London, England.

British Library Cataloguing in Publication Data.
A CIP record for this book is available from the British Library.

Designed and typeset by Triple Gem Press
in 10/13 Charter.

Printed and donated for free distribution by
The Corporate Body of the Buddha Educational Foundation
11F., 55 Hang Chow South Road Sec 1, Taipei, Taiwan, R.O.C.
Tel: 886-2-23951198 , Fax: 886-2-23913415
Email: overseas@budaedu.org
Website:http://www.budaedu.org

Printed in Taiwan

Contents

Preface

This book was written in Thailand where I lived for some years. When I got to know the Thai people, I was impressed by their generosity. In Thailand one meets many people who do not set a limit to their generosity, be they rich or poor, and one is inspired to be more generous oneself. When one meets the Thais one notices their sincerity, their tolerance and their wise attitude towards the problems of life. I was also impressed by the earnestness and dedication of the monks who lead a life of simplicity, "contented with little", and who try to realize the Buddhist teachings in their daily lives. When I visited the temples in Thailand, I saw Buddhism being lived in daily life.

And so, I wanted to study Buddhism. We are inclined to think that Buddhism is only a religion for people living in an oriental culture, but when we learn more about it, we see that it is completely different from what we first thought. We learn that it is in fact a "way of life" which makes for the well-being and happiness of all people, no matter what their nationality.

Through the study of the Buddha's teachings, which are also called the "Dhamma", we learn to develop the wisdom which leads to detachment from the "self" and finally to the eradication of greed, hatred and ignorance. When there is less attachment in our life, there is more room for unselfish loving kindness (mettā) and compassion (karuṇā) for all living beings.

The way one has to follow in order to develop this wisdom is the "eightfold Path". Through the development of the eightfold Path we come to know better the phenomena within and around ourselves; these phenomena can be experienced through the six doorways of eyes, ears, nose, tongue, body-sense and mind. They are continually susceptible to change and they are impermanent. What we take for "I" or "self" all the time does not exist; there are only phenomena which arise and fall away again.

In Thailand I experienced that "to reside in a suitable location is the greatest blessing" (Mahā-Mangala Sutta). Thailand was the country where I met the "wise person" who helped me to understand the Buddhist teachings and who showed me the way to develop the eightfold Path. It is a great blessing to live in a country where Buddhism is taught and practised so that one can acquire not only theoretical knowledge of Buddhism, but also the way leading to the realization of the Buddha's teachings in daily life.

The Buddha, who attained enlightenment and who had clear comprehension of everything which is real, left us his teachings which are now in the form of the *Tipiṭaka* (three "baskets"), the three parts of the Buddhist scriptures, consisting of the *Vinaya*, the Book of Discipline for the monks, the *Suttanta*, Discourses, and the *Abhidhamma*, the "higher teachings" or exposition of realities in detail. The Buddhist teachings themselves should be our guide in the practice. Some people want to apply themselves to "meditation" immediately without first studying the teachings and thus they do not know which result their way of mental development will bring. The Buddhist teachings are so subtle; one needs to study them thoroughly and to consider them carefully in order to understand what the Buddha taught about mental development. Mental development includes both the development of calm (samatha) and the development of insight (vipassanā), but they each have a different way of practice and a different result. If one does not follow the Buddha's way, but follows rather one's own or someone else's way, one cannot reach the goal.

In this book I do not pretend to give a complete outline of the Buddha's teachings. My purpose is to draw the reader to the Buddhist scriptures themselves and to the practice in accordance with the teachings. I want to ask the reader to read this book with discrimination and to investigate for himself or herself what the Buddhist scriptures say. By our own practice we can prove whether the way we follow is the right one for the goal we have chosen. If we intend to develop insight, vipassanā, the result should be that we gain more understanding of the realities which appear at the present moment through the five senses and the mind, and less clinging to the concept of "self". In the final analysis, the reader will have to find out for himself and to decide for himself about the path he wants to follow in his life.

I feel deep gratitude to Miss Sujin Boriharnwanaket who helped me to understand the Buddhist teachings and who showed me the way to develop vipassanā in daily life. The writing of this book would not have been possible without her help and valuable advice.

Buddhism in Daily Life originated from a compilation of lectures for a Buddhist radio programme in English which were printed and reprinted in Thailand several times. Formerly this book was printed in two volumes with the titles *Buddhist Outlook on Daily Life* (now Part I) and *Mental Development in Daily Life* (now Part II). Jonathan Abbot and Susie Whitmore were of great assistance in preparing the text of these two volumes. This present edition has been reprinted in England after there were some requests from English people. I want to acknowledge my appreciation to the "Dhamma Study and Propagation Foundation"; to the sponsors of the printing of this edition, Asoka Jayasundera and family, Anura Perrera and family and Laksham Perera and family; and to the publisher Alan Weller. Thanks to their assistance the reprinting of this book has been made possible. I wrote *Buddhism in Daily Life* a long time ago and I have since written *Abhidhamma in Daily Life, The World in the Buddhist Sense* and *The Buddha's Path*. The last book gives a more complete outline of the Buddha's teachings for people in Western countries who may not have had an opportunity to study Buddhism and who may find it difficult to grasp the core of the teachings. *Buddhism in Daily Life* reflects my own experiences when I first came into contact with Buddhism in Thailand and became deeply impressed by the Buddha's teachings.

For the quotations from the Buddhist scriptures, I have used mostly the English translation of the Pali Text Society[1]. For the quotations from the *Path of Purification* (Visuddhimagga), I have used the translation by Bhikkhu Ñāṇamoli (Colombo, Sri Lanka, 1964). The *Path of Purification* is an Encyclopedia on Buddhism which is a compilation of ancient commentarial material arranged by the commentator Buddhaghosa in the fifth century A.D.

The chapters which I wrote in the form of question and answer were inspired by real questions posed by people who were confronted with many problems in the practice of vipassanā. They were posed by myself as well. I found from my own experience

[1] The translations are available at the Pali Text Society, 73 Lime Walk, Headington, Oxford OX3 7AD, England.

that the practice of vipassanā is very subtle; that the clinging to the notion of "self" and the desire for results can easily lead us astray, that they can cause us to follow the wrong path instead of the right path.

When I wrote *Buddhism in Daily Life* I thought of the many people who want to know the truth about themselves. I find Dhamma the greatest blessing in life and I want to share with others what I learnt from the Buddhist teachings and from the practice of the Dhamma in daily life. I hope that this book can help others to find the Path that leads to real peace.

May the Dhamma be the greatest blessing in our lives,

Nina van Gorkom

Chapter 1

General Aspects of Buddhism

Questioner: What led you to the study of the Buddha's teachings?

Nina: When I first came to Thailand I was naturally interested in knowing more about the Thai people. I wanted to learn more about their customs and their way of thinking. I found the study of Buddhism essential for the understanding of the Thai culture because the spiritual background of the Thai people is Buddhism.

Therefore I started to study Buddhism and the more I studied, the more I found my interest growing. When one is in Thailand one should take the opportunity to study Buddhism and to try to understand the practice of Buddhism as well. Deep understanding will not come from books alone. Understanding is developed above all by the practice, by the application of the Buddhist teachings in daily life!

Question: Would you tell me what you mean by the practice of Buddhism in daily life?

Nina: One is first confronted with the practice of Buddhism when one sees different customs of the Thais, such as giving food to the monks, paying respect to the Buddha image or reciting the "precepts" on special occasions such as "Uposatha Day"[1].

In the beginning I thought that these customs were mixed with many things which are not essential for the practice of Buddhism. For example, I did not see how the presenting of eggs to the statue of the "Emerald Buddha" could have anything to do with the practice of Buddhism. However, even such popular beliefs can teach us something about the practice of Buddhism.

There are many levels of understanding the Buddha's teachings. The people who present eggs to the statue of the Buddha express their confidence in him. This is a wholesome act which will bear its fruit accordingly. However, the people who present the eggs

[1] A day of vigil or fasting which laypeople may observe four times a month (the days of the new moon, full moon and the two days of the half moon) by undertaking moral precepts and by visiting the temple.

may not realize that it is their respect to the Buddha which will bring them a good result and not the eggs presented to him. They may not clearly see which cause will bring them which result. They would receive greater benefit from their act of paying respect to the Buddha if this were done in a more meaningful way. They could, for example, pay respect to the Buddha by abstaining from ill deeds, in serving other people, in learning more about the teachings of the Buddha and in helping other people to understand the teachings as well.

Question: Could you tell me more about the different degrees of understanding the Buddha's teaching?

Nina: As regards paying respect to the Buddha image, people who have a higher level of understanding know that the Buddha has passed away completely. When one has studied the teachings more deeply and when one has tried to verify them in daily life, one understands that, although the Buddha has passed away, it still makes sense to pay respect to him. It is the wholesome mental state of the person who pays respect to the Buddha or who offers something to him which will bring its result accordingly. Every good action brings a good result to the person who performs it. One reaps what one has sown.

The person who pays respect to the Buddha with the right understanding does not have a confused idea of a Buddha in heaven who could see him or hear him. The image of the Buddha reminds him of the virtues of the Buddha. He thinks of the wisdom of the Buddha who found the Path to complete freedom from sorrow all by himself and who was able to help other people as well to find this Path. He thinks of the purity of the Buddha, of the purity in all his deeds, his speech and his thoughts. He thinks of the compassion of the Buddha, who taught out of compassion for everybody.

Question: What is the meaning of giving food to the monks?

Nina: As regards the giving of food to the monks, some people doubt whether that is of any use. They are inclined to think that monks want to have an easy life and that they do not have to work at all, but they forget that the real meaning of being a monk is seeking the truth.

A monk's life is a hard life, he does not have a family life, he cannot choose his own food and he does not take part in any entertainment such as going to the movies or football matches. He renounces the luxuries of a home, entertainment, choice of clothing and food, in order to seek the truth and to help other people to find the truth as well.

When people give food to the monks their act is one which will be fruitful for both parties. The giver will benefit from his act because he has a wholesome mental state at the time of giving: when there is generosity there is no greed or attachment. The receiver will benefit from the act of the giver because he is encouraged to study and practise the Buddhist teachings more earnestly and to help other people to know the teachings as well. He knows that the food he receives puts him under an obligation to be worthy of the gift, to work for the spiritual welfare of the whole world. Monks are continually reminded of their responsibility as monks, and twice a month they recite the rules of "Pāṭimokkha" in which their obligations are summed up. Furthermore, when the receiver is aware of the wholesome state of the giver, he will rejoice in the good deeds of the giver and thus he will have a wholesome mental state as well; he will be inspired by the generosity of the giver.

Question: Do you not find it difficult to think in terms of "mental states"? Thinking of one's own mental state might seem an ego-centric attitude.

Nina: Thinking of one's own mental states is very realistic, because it is the different mental states which make us act in this way or that. Only if we study our mental states and the many factors which cause them to be like this or that, will we be able to understand the deepest motives of our behaviour. We have to start by being aware of our own mental states. This is not egocentric, because we have to understand ourselves first, before we can understand other people.

Through the study of the *Abhidhamma* one can begin to have more understanding of one's own mental states. The Abhidhamma is that part of the Buddhist teachings which analyses the different states of mind and which explains in detail about everything which is real. The study of the Abhidhamma helps us to understand which causes bring which effects in our life and in the lives of other people.

Question: Do you find that you can verify the Abhidhamma in your daily life?

Nina: It was a great discovery for me to find that the Abhidhamma can be verified in daily life, although one can in the beginning experience only part of the realities the Abhidhamma explains.

At first one might think that the Abhidhamma is too subtle and one might doubt whether it is useful to study the many different degrees of ignorance and wisdom, but one learns that each of these different degrees brings its corresponding result.

In studying the Abhidhamma one learns to understand more about other people as well. One learns that people are different because of different accumulations of experiences in the past. Because of these different accumulations people behave differently. At each moment one accumulates new experiences and this conditions what one will be like and what one will experience in the future.

When we understand more about the different accumulations of different people, we are less inclined to judge other people. When we see people paying respect to the Buddha with apparently very little understanding we know that their accumulations are thus and that they are performing a wholesome act according to their ability.

Question: Do you think that a person with very little understanding can ever reach a level of higher understanding? In other words, when one's accumulations have conditioned one's character, is there anything that can be done about it? Is it possible to improve one's degree of understanding?

Nina: Everything can be done about it: wisdom can be developed very gradually and thus one's accumulations can be changed. Those who have a higher level of understanding can and should help other people to develop a higher level of understanding as well.

I shall give an example. Children can become novices. They share the life of the monks in order to learn more about the Buddhist teachings and to make merit for their parents who can rejoice in their good deeds. Many people think that the person who makes merit can literally transfer his own good deeds to other people, dead or alive. This is not the right understanding. It is not possible to transfer merit to other people, because everyone will receive the result of his own deeds. Older monks who have reached a higher level of understanding can help the novices to have more understanding about the wholesome act they are performing. If they could understand correctly the meaning of the merit they make, their renunciation would be even more fruitful. The novices are performing a very wholesome act in renouncing the company of their relatives in order to study the Buddhist teachings and to train themselves in the precepts, which are moral rules. This gives them a good spiritual foundation for their whole life. They will receive the fruit of this wholesome act themselves. The merit they make cannot literally be transferred to other people. However, other people, no matter whether they are deceased or still alive, can have wholesome states of mind inspired by the good deeds of someone else. Their own wholesome mental states will bring them a wholesome result. So parents, even deceased parents, if they are in planes of existence where they can rejoice in the good deeds of their child, may have wholesome states of mind and these will bring wholesome results in the future. The expression "transfer of merit" is a misleading one, because it does not give us the understanding of the real cause and effect.

Question: You used the expression "mental state". Could you explain what it means? I would like to ask you in general whether you find the English language adequate to render the real meaning of the realities which are described in the Abhidhamma.

Nina: The English language is not adequate to render the meaning of the realities described in the Abhidhamma. The "Three Collections" of the teachings (Tipiṭaka) use Pāli terms, and therefore it is better to learn the Pāli terms and their meaning. For instance, the word "mental state" which is a translation of the Pāli term "citta"[1], is misleading. "State" implies something which stays for some time, be it short or long. However, each mental state or citta falls away immediately, as soon as it has arisen, to be succeeded by the next citta. This happens more rapidly than a lightning flash. The different cittas succeed one another so rapidly that it seems that there is only one citta. That is the reason why people take a citta for "self".

For the same reason the word "mind" gives us a wrong idea of

[1] Pronounce: chitta.

reality. We often hear the expression "mastering one's mind" or "controlling one's mind". Many people think that the mind is something static which can be grasped and controlled. There are many different cittas, none of which can be considered as "self" or as belonging to a "self".

In the *Lesser Discourse to Saccaka*(Middle Length Sayings I, no. 35) we read that the Buddha asked Saccaka whether he could be master of his body or of his mind, just as a king rules over his subjects. The Buddha asked: "When you speak thus: 'The body is myself,' have you power over this body of yours (and can you say), 'Let my body be thus, let my body be not thus'?" The Buddha asked the same question about the mind. Saccaka who was at first silent finally had to agree that it was not possible.

In daily life we can find out that the Buddha spoke the truth. If we were masters of our body we would not grow older, there would not be sickness and we would not die. However, old age, sickness and death are unavoidable.

Neither can we be masters of our mind; the mental states which arise are beyond control. Like and dislike are beyond control, they arise when there are conditions. When we eat food which is prepared to our taste, we cannot help liking it. If someone insults us, we cannot help feeling aversion; we may reason later and try to understand the other person, but we cannot help feeling aversion at first. Like, dislike, and even reasoning about our likes and dislikes, are not "self", they are different mental states which arise when there are the right conditions.

We all are inclined to take mental states for "self"; for example, when we enjoy something we take our enjoyment for "self". However, the next moment there could be aversion, and we might wonder where the enjoyment which we took for "self" has gone.

It is very human to like the idea of a "self" and to hold on to it. The Buddha knew this and therefore, after his enlightenment, he felt for a moment inclined not to teach other people the Path he had found. However, the Buddha knew also that people have different levels of understanding. We read in the *Kindred Sayings* (I, Ch. VI, The Brahmā Suttas, Ch. 1, §1, The Entreaty) that the Buddha surveyed the world with his "Buddha-vision" and saw people with different levels of understanding, some of whom would be able to understand his teaching:

> *As in a pool of blue or red or white lotus, some lotus plants born in the water, emerge not, but grow up and thrive sunken beneath the surface; and other lotus plants, born in the water and growing up in the water rise to the surface; and other lotus plants, born in the water and growing up in the water, stand thrusting themselves above the water and are unwetted by it; even so did the Exalted One look down over the world with a Buddha's Eye and see beings whose eyes were scarcely dimmed by dust, beings whose eyes were sorely dimmed by dust, beings sharp of sense and blunted of sense, beings of good and beings of evil disposition, beings docile and beings indocile, some among them living with a perception of the danger of other worlds[1] and of wrong doing.*

Therefore the Buddha decided to make known the Path he had discovered.

Question: People have different accumulations. They are conditioned in many ways. We have used the word "condition" several times already. Could you explain the meaning of this term?

Nina: I will give an example from daily life. My husband comes home from his office, feeling tired and somewhat irritated. I tell him something amusing which has happened and he laughs and feels happy again. Thus one can notice that there are different cittas[2], and that each citta has its own conditions. The amount of work at the office is a condition for my husband's tiredness and irritation. Afterwards there is another condition which makes him feel happy again.

Cittas are conditioned and each citta accumulates a new experience, which will condition cittas in the future. Everybody accumulates different tastes, abilities, likes and dislikes. One cannot always know the conditions which make people behave in this or in that way, but sometimes it is possible to know. For instance, people are addicted to different things, some of which are very harmful, others less so. One's education and the surroundings in which one is living can be a condition for these addictions. In some countries or regions it is the custom to drink an enormous amount of coffee the whole day and people even give coffee to

[1] Namely in rebirth.

[2] Moment of consciousness or "mental state".

very small children. Thus one acquires the taste for coffee from one's youth. As regards attachment to alcoholic drinks, there must be a condition for that as well. One starts with a little drink every day and gradually one's attachment increases.

Everybody should find out for himself how much attachment he accumulates and whether this brings him happiness or sorrow.

Question: There is not anything which one can control. Even each citta which arises because of conditions falls away immediately, to be succeeded by the next citta. It seems as if the situation is hopeless. Could you tell me whether something can be done to walk the right way in life?

Nina: The situation is not hopeless. Wisdom, the understanding of reality, can condition one to have more wholesome mental states and to do good deeds.

There is no "self" who can suppress one's bad inclinations; there is no "self" who can force one to do good deeds. Everybody can verify this in daily life. For example, if we tell ourselves: "today I will be very kind to everybody", can we prevent ourselves from suddenly saying an unkind word? Most of the time it has happened before we realize it.

If we are able to suppress our anger for a while we are inclined to think that there is a "self" who can suppress anger. In reality there are at that moment cittas which are not conditioned by anger, but which arise from other conditions. Afterwards there will be anger again because anger is not really eradicated by suppression. Only wisdom, seeing things as they are, can very gradually eradicate everything which is unwholesome in us.

We can develop this wisdom step by step. Even wisdom is not "self"; it can only arise when there are the right conditions. We can develop wisdom by knowing through direct experience the mental phenomena and physical phenomena in and around ourselves. When we have realized that none of these mental and physical phenomena stays or is permanent, we will understand that we cannot take any phenomenon for "self".

The Buddha explained to his disciples that it is "comprehending", seeing things as they are, which will eradicate unwholesomeness. When we are still learning to develop wisdom and when we notice that we have unwholesome cittas, we are troubled about it, we have aversion because of it. He whose wisdom is developed, has right understanding of his life. He knows that there is no "self", and that everything arises because of conditions. Thus he is not troubled, he is simply aware of the present moment.

The word "comprehending" is used in the suttas many times. This should help us to see that we do not have to perform extraordinary deeds; we should learn to be aware of the present moment in order to see things as they are. Of course wisdom cannot be fully developed in one day. For a long time we have been used to the idea of "self". In conventional language we have to use the words "I" and "self" continually in order to make ourselves understood.

Question: So wisdom is wholesome, and not understanding things as they are is unwholesome and brings unhappiness. Do you find that you can verify this in daily life?

Nina: Yes. I will give an example. We are constantly taking our body for "self", although we know that it does not last. Thus, when we suffer from sickness or pain, or when we become old, we attach so much importance to these facts that we feel quite oppressed by them. If one of our sense-organs does not function or if we become an invalid, we feel we are the most unhappy person in the world. Attachment to our body only brings sorrow, whereas if we would see things as they are, there would be less sorrow for us.

If one wants to see the body as it really is, one should distinguish the body from mentality. It is true that in this world body and mentality condition each other. However, one should know the different characteristics of each, so that they can be experienced as they are.

The same elements which constitute dead matter constitute the body as well. Both dead matter and the body are composed of the *element of earth* or solidity, the *element of water* or cohesion, the *element of fire* or temperature and the *element of wind* or motion[1]. One is inclined to think: "Is there not a soul which makes the body alive and is the body therefore not different from dead matter?" There is no soul; there are only physical phenomena and mental phenomena which arise and fall away all the time. We are not used to distinguishing the body from the mind and

[1] These terms do not stand for the conventional ideas of earth, water, fire and wind, but they denote characteristics of realities.

analysing them as to what they really are. However, this is necessary if we want to know reality.

The body itself does not know anything; in this respect it is the same as dead matter. If we can see that the body is only a composition of physical phenomena which arise and fall away completely, and not "self", and that the mind is a series of mental phenomena which arise and fall away and not "self", the veil of ignorance will fall from our eyes.

If we try to develop this understanding we can see for ourselves what the result is. We can find out whether this understanding brings us more freedom from attachment or not. Attachment brings sorrow.

The Buddha taught people to see things as they are. We do not have to fast or to be an ascetic. It is our duty to look after the body and to feed it. The Buddha taught the "Middle Way": one does not have to force oneself to undertake difficult practices, but on the other hand one should learn through right understanding to become detached from the things in an around oneself. Just understanding, seeing things as they are, that is the "Middle Way".

Question: So, seeing things as they are is the practice of vipassanā, insight. Most people think that it is a complicated form of meditation which can be learnt only in a meditation centre. That is the reason why most people will not even try it. But from our conversation it appears that vipassanā is seeing the things of our daily life as they are. Do you find that one has to have much theoretical knowledge before one starts the practice of vipassanā?

Nina: The word "meditation" frightens many people; they think that it must be very complicated. But in reality one does not have to do anything special. If one wants to develop vipassanā one needs some theoretical knowledge. One does not have to know about all physical elements and mental elements in detail, but one should know that the body is made up of physical elements and that these are different from mental elements. There are many different physical elements and these elements are continually changing. One should know that there are many different mental elements: one citta arises and falls away, then the next citta arises and falls away. Cittas arise and fall away successively, one at a time. Seeing is one citta, hearing is another citta, thinking is again another citta, they are all different cittas.

Developing vipassanā does not mean that one has to be aware of all those different elements at each moment; that would not be possible. Nor does one have to do anything special; one can perform all the activities of one's daily life. One gradually begins to understand that there are only physical phenomena and mental phenomena and one begins to be aware of these phenomena quite naturally, without having to force oneself, because they are there all the time.

When we understand that these phenomena can be known as they are only through direct awareness of them, awareness will arise by itself little by little. We will experience that awareness will arise when there are the right conditions. It does not matter if there is not a great deal of awareness in the beginning. It is important to understand that awareness is not "self" either, but a mental phenomenon which arises when there are the right conditions. We cannot force awareness to arise.

In understanding more about physical phenomena and mental phenomena, and in being aware of them in daily life, wisdom will develop. Thus there will be more wholesomeness and less unwholesomeness.

Question: Do you find that awareness in this way brings you happiness?

Nina: When there is understanding of what things really are, there will be more wholesomeness in our life. There will be less clinging to the concept of "self" when we perform good deeds, and thus good deeds will be purer. We do not refrain from evil things because we have to follow certain rules, but because we have more understanding as to which causes bring which effects.

The right understanding of what things are will very gradually eradicate unwholesomeness. When there is less unwholesomeness there will be more peace in life.

Everybody should verify this for himself!

Chapter 2

Right Understanding in Daily Life

What is the effect of the Buddha's teachings on people's actions? In what way could the Buddha's teachings effectively help people to perform wholesome deeds? Is it possible to do good deeds because a person with authority tells us: "Be detached and do good deeds"?

From experience we know that a good example might help to some extent, but the source of the good deeds is within ourselves: our mentality determines our actions. If someone wants to do his utmost to help other people he should understand himself first. He should understand the causes which make him act in this or in that way. If he develops right understanding of these causes he will be able to lead a more wholesome life and to help other people in the most effective way.

Mentality is the source from which deeds spring; it is therefore not possible to determine the degree of wholesomeness from the outward appearance of deeds alone. There are many gradations of wholesomeness depending on the mentality which motivates a good deed.

Some people give money to needy people, but that does not mean that there may not still be conceit or other selfish motives. Others give without conceit, but they may still have attachment: they give only to people they like. There are people who give out of pure loving-kindness, without any thought of attachment. This is a more wholesome way of giving.

We may wonder whether the study of so many details is necessary. In daily life we will see that it is very helpful to know the different kinds of citta and to know which citta motivates which kind of action. Cittas change all the time, succeeding each other very rapidly. If we learn to distinguish different kinds of citta, we will see that even while we are performing a wholesome deed, unwholesome cittas can follow very closely upon the wholesome cittas.

"Wholesome" is the translation of the Pāli term "kusala". A

wholesome deed in its widest sense means a deed which brings no harm to oneself nor to other people at the moment the deed is done or later on.

In the *Discourse on the Foreign Cloth*(Middle Length Sayings II, no. 88) we read about wholesome deeds, wholesome speech and wholesome thoughts. King Pasenadi questions Ānanda about the nature of unwholesome and wholesome deeds. As to wholesome or "skilled" bodily conduct we read the following conversation:

> *"But what, revered sir, is skilled bodily conduct?"*
>
> *"Whatever the bodily conduct, sire, that has no blemish."*
>
> *"But what, revered sir, is the bodily conduct that has no blemish?"*
>
> *"Whatever the bodily conduct, sire, that is non-injurious."*
>
> *"And what, revered sir, is the bodily conduct that is non-injurious?"*
>
> *"Whatever the bodily conduct, sire, that is joyous in result."*
>
> *"And what, revered sir, is the bodily conduct that is joyous in result?"*
>
> *"Whatever bodily conduct, sire, does not conduce to the torment of self and does not conduce to the torment of others and does not conduce to the torment of both, and by which the unskilled states dwindle away, the skilled states increase much...."*

The same is said about wholesome speech and wholesome thinking. These words render the meaning of wholesome or "kusala" in its widest sense. There are many kinds and intensities of kusala. In developing "right understanding" or wisdom there can be kusala of a higher degree.

Wisdom or understanding is a translation of the Pāli term "paññā". Paññā does not only mean knowledge acquired from the study of books, paññā also includes insight, right understanding of the realities of daily life. Paññā can be developed in daily life. When paññā accompanies kusala citta, wholesome citta, there is a higher degree of wholesomeness. There are many degrees of paññā and each degree brings its result accordingly.

It is a typical Buddhist approach to investigate and to be aware of the different mental phenomena and physical phenomena which can be experienced through eyes, ears, nose, tongue, bodysense and mind. If one is not used to this approach one might feel somewhat bewildered at first. However, after we have investigated more these mental and physical phenomena, we will find out that only thus it is possible to understand the different ways in which we ourselves and other people behave, and to know which causes bring which effects in life. It makes no sense to speak in vague, general terms about realities, because the real understanding of our experiences in life can never be developed in that way.

Someone told me about a monk who was preaching in a way which was of great help to people in their daily lives. When I asked what the monk was preaching, the answer was that he was speaking about "citcai". "Citcai"[1] is the word in Thai for "state of mind", in Pāli: citta. This monk had the right approach to life. One should follow the example of the Buddha; one should not only tell people to do good deeds, but one should teach them as well how to do good deeds. In order to know how to do good deeds, we should go back to the source of the good deeds: the mental states or "cittas". It is preferable to use the Pāli term "citta" rather than a translation from the Pāli since translations do not render the meaning of the terms adequately. For example, the English translation of "citta" as "state of mind" or "mental state" implies something which stays, which does not change. But this is not the characteristic of citta. When we have learned more about cittas we will find out that there is no citta which stays, even for a second. Each citta which arises falls away immediately, to be succeeded by the next citta. Cittas determine our life and the lives of other people; they condition the actions we perform in life.

Many people are not used to this approach; they are used to looking at the outward appearance of things. Scientists are very advanced in the study of outer space, but little is known about what goes on inwardly in man. People are used to paying attention to the things they see and hear, but they are not used to attending to seeing-consciousness and to hearing-consciousness. They do not think of the cittas which perform the functions of seeing and hearing.

Seeing-consciousness and hearing-consciousness are realities and therefore it is important to know more about them. That part of the Buddhist teachings which analyses and explains in detail mental phenomena and physical phenomena is called the "Abhidhamma".

[1] Pronounce: chitchai.

The Abhidhamma deals with everything which is real. Studying the Abhidhamma can change one's life.

Many Thais listen to lectures about Abhidhamma, and not only those who have been educated at a college or university, but also those who have never received a higher education. I have heard of cases in which the study of different cittas has helped people to lead a more wholesome life. I heard of someone who was at first inclined to have feelings of revenge towards other people, but who was gradually able to overcome those feelings by understanding what those feelings were. Many Thais know about the realities taught in the Abhidhamma, and they are able to apply their knowledge in daily life. Foreigners do not usually hear about this because people do not often speak about Abhidhamma to foreigners.

Unwholesome mental states or "akusala cittas" and wholesome mental states or "kusala cittas" are realities of daily life. In order to know more about these realities we should try to understand ourselves first: if we do not understand ourselves we cannot help other people. This does not mean, however, that we have to wait our whole life before we can start helping other people. Even those who are just beginning to understand things as they are can help others to have right understanding too.

Paññā, wisdom or understanding, is the opposite of ignorance, the root of all defilement and sorrow. Paññā is important for the development of kusala cittas. It is possible to do good deeds without paññā, but if there is understanding of what is unwholesome and what is wholesome, and understanding of what the result is of unwholesome and wholesome deeds, one is able to lead a more wholesome life. Thus, the development of paññā is of great benefit both to ourselves and to others.

There are many degrees of paññā. When a teacher explains to his pupils that kusala cittas with gratitude or honesty will bring a pleasant result and that unwholesome deeds motivated by greed or anger will bring an unpleasant result, the explanation may be the condition for them to have some degree of paññā. With paññā they may be able to develop kusala cittas and to perform more wholesome deeds.

There is a higher degree of paññā when people realize the impermanence of all the things they enjoy in life. When people see how short human life is, they will try not to be attached too much to the pleasant things of life. This understanding will stimulate them to a greater generosity and to more readiness to help other people. They will be less selfish.

Some people who have this degree of paññā might change their way of life and live contentedly without any luxury. Others might decide to "go forth from home into homelessness"; they might decide to become a monk. A monk's life is not an easy life. He lives without family and is one who is "contented with little". In the *Discourse on the Sixfold Cleansing*(Middle Length Sayings III, no. 112) we read that the Buddha spoke about the monk who told of his renunciation of the world:

> *"So I, your reverences, after a time, getting rid of my wealth, whether small or great, getting rid of my circle of relations, whether small or great, having cut off my hair and beard, having put on saffron robes, went forth from home into homelessness...."*

The Buddha explained that people are too much attached to the sense-impressions received through eyes, ears, nose, tongue and body. He spoke about the "five strands of sense-pleasures". We read in the *Discourse with Subha*(Middle Length Sayings II, no. 99) that the Buddha spoke with Subha about the five strands of sense-pleasures:

> *... These five, brahman youth, are the strands of pleasures of the senses. What five? Material shapes cognisable by the eye, agreeable, pleasant, liked, enticing, connected with sensual pleasures, alluring. Sounds cognisable by the ear... Smells cognisable by the nose... Tastes cognisable by the tongue... Touches cognisable by the body, agreeable, pleasant, liked, enticing, connected with sensual pleasures, alluring. These, brahman youth, are the five strands of sense-pleasures. Brahman youth, the brahman Pokkharasāti of the Upamañña (clan) of the Subhaga forest glade, is enslaved and infatuated by these five strands of sense-pleasures, he is addicted to them, and enjoys them without seeing the peril (in them), without knowing the escape (from them)....*

We would like to have pleasant sense-impressions and we are inclined to attach too much importance to them. We are so absorbed in what we see or hear that we forget that sense-impressions are not true happiness. In the *Discourse to Māgandiya*(Middle Length Sayings II, no. 75) we read that the Buddha said to Māgandiya:

> *Now I, Māgandiya, when I was formerly a householder, endowed and provided with the five strands of sense-pleasures, revelled in them... But after a time, having known the coming to be and passing away of sense-pleasures and the satisfaction and peril of them and the escape as it really is, getting rid of the craving for sense-pleasures, suppressing the fever for sense-pleasures, I dwelt devoid of thirst, my mind inwardly calmed. I saw other beings not yet devoid of attachment to sense-pleasures who were pursuing sense-pleasures (although) they were being consumed by craving for sense-pleasures, burning with the fever for sense-pleasures. I did not envy them: I had no delight therein....*

People who understand that there is a higher happiness than the pleasures which one can enjoy through the five senses might apply themselves to the development of calm or "samatha". The calm which is developed in samatha is temporary freedom from attachment, anger and other defilements. There are several meditation subjects of samatha, such as recollection of the Buddha's virtues, mindfulness of breathing or loving-kindness. It depends on a person's accumulations which subject conditions calm for him. Samatha is not a matter of just trying to concentrate on an object. Most important is right understanding of the meditation subject and of the way to attain the calm which is wholesome by means of the meditation subject. If one does not know the difference between kusala citta and akusala citta one is likely to take attachment to silence for kusala and then samatha cannot be developed. One has to know the characteristic of calm which is wholesome, free from akusala. Then there can be conditions for more calm. Calm in samatha can reach such a high degree that one becomes totally absorbed in the meditation subject. There are different stages of this calm absorption or "jhāna". During jhāna one does not receive impressions through the five senses and thus one is at those moments not enslaved to them. One enjoys a higher happiness. In higher stages of jhāna one attains a greater tranquillity of mind until one no longer feels rapture or joy; one transcends happy feeling and there is equanimity instead. When, however, the citta is not jhānacitta, there are sense-impressions again.

Samatha is a means for the cultivation of wholesomeness. People who apply themselves to samatha may become very peaceful and amiable. They can be of great comfort to people who are restless. However, in samatha defilements are not eradicated. Although one is not enslaved to sense-impressions during the time of jhāna, one still clings to them when the citta is no longer jhānacitta. The jhānas do not last; they are impermanent. Moreoever, there is a more subtle form of clinging, a clinging to the happiness of the jhānas. One might think that one is without clinging when one does not indulge in sense-pleasures. However, one might still cling to the joy of jhāna which is not associated with sense-pleasures, one might cling to pleasant feeling or equanimity which can accompany jhānacitta.

For the development of samatha paññā is necessary, but this kind of paññā cannot eradicate defilements. There is a higher paññā which can eradicate all defilements, even the most subtle forms of clinging. This paññā is developed in "insight meditation" or "vipassanā". In vipassanā, paññā gradually eliminates ignorance, the root of all defilements. One learns more about the realities which present themselves through eyes, ears, nose, tongue, body-sense and mind at any moment. We know so little about the most common things of daily life. How often are we aware of bodily movements during the day? How often are we aware of bodily phenomena such as hardness or softness while we are stretching or bending our arms, or when we are moving our lips while talking? We do not really know what sound is, what hearing is or what it is we take for "self" while hearing. We do not know the phenomena which appear at the present moment.

When we are absorbed in the outer appearance and the details of things, we will not be able to be aware of the realities of the present moment. So long as we are carried away by like or dislike of what we see and hear, it is impossible to see things as they are. It is as if we are asleep; we are not yet awake to the truth. The Buddha was perfectly mindful and he had complete knowledge of all the different kinds of mental and physical phenomena. Therefore he could call himself "the Awakened One"; he was fully awake to the truth. We, too, should wake up to the truth.

In vipassanā, paññā will gradually develop and it will know things as they are. In being aware of the reality which appears at the present moment we learn that there are two kinds of reality: physical phenomena or *rūpa* and mental phenomena or *nāma*. Rūpa does not know anything whereas nāma experiences something; it experiences an object. For example, visible object is rūpa; it does not know anything. Seeing is a type of nāma; it experiences an object: visible object. Hearing and thinking are other types of nāma, different from seeing. There are many different types of nāma and rūpa, and in vipassanā we learn to experience their characteristics.

In the development of vipassanā the impermanence of nāmas and rūpas will be directly known. One may have reflected before on the impermanence of all things in life. Reflection on the truth is necessary, but it is not the same as the direct knowledge of the impermanence of all realities in and around oneself. In the beginning the arising and falling away of nāma and rūpa cannot be realised. However, if we learn to be aware of different characteristics of nāma and rūpa which appear one at a time, and if we realize that each nāma or rūpa which appears now is different from preceding nāmas and rūpas, we will be less inclined to think that nāma and rūpa last, and we will be less inclined to take them for "self".

In the *Greater Discourse of a Full Moon*(Middle Length Sayings III, no. 109) we read that the Buddha, while he was staying near Sāvatthī in the palace of Migāra's mother in the Eastern Monastery, said to the monks:

> *"... What do you think about this, monks? Is material shape permanent or impermanent?"*
>
> *"Impermanent, revered sir."*
>
> *"But is what is impermanent painful or is it pleasant?"*
>
> *"Painful, revered sir."*
>
> *"And is it right to regard that which is impermanent, suffering, liable to change, as 'This is mine, this am I, this is myself'?"*
>
> *"No, revered sir."*

The Buddha asked the same about mental phenomena.

In the *Discourse on Mindfulness of the Body*(Middle Length

Sayings, III, no. 119) we read that the Buddha, when he was staying near Sāvatthī, at the Jeta Grove, spoke to the monks about mindfulness of the body and the advantages of it. Some of these are the following:

> *... He is one who overcomes dislike and liking, and dislike (and liking) do not overcome him; he fares along constantly conquering any dislike (and liking) that have arisen. He is one who overcomes fear and dread, and fear and dread do not overcome him; and he fares along constantly conquering any fear and dread that have arisen. He is one who bears cold, heat, hunger, thirst, the touch of gadfly, mosquito, wind and sun, creeping things, ways of speech that are irksome, unwelcome; he is of a character to bear bodily feelings which, arising, are painful, acute, sharp, shooting, disagreeable, miserable, deadly....*

We will gradually learn to give in less to attachment and to anger or aversion when we have realized that these are only different types of nāma which arise because of conditions and then fall away again immediately.

We should not wait to develop insight, right understanding of realities, until we are old or have retired from our work. When we develop this wisdom we will know ourselves better, we will be aware more often of the moments of akusala cittas which arise, even while we are doing good deeds. Conceit about our good deeds may arise or we may expect something in return for our good deeds, such as praise or a good name. When we gradually see more clearly that there are only nāma and rūpa which arise because of conditions, there will eventually be less clinging to a concept of self who performs kusala or akusala. When there is less clinging to the self good deeds will become purer. The paññā developed in vipassanā is the "Right Understanding" of the eightfold Path which leads to nibbāna. Everyone has to tread this Path by himself. One can only purify oneself. One cannot be purified by other people; other people can only help one to find the right Path. There will be no lasting world peace so long as there is craving, ill-will and ignorance. It is very necessary to take part of the world organisations which promote the peace and the welfare of nations, and to give material aid to those who are in need. However, we should realize that this is not enough, that it will only help to a certain degree. The real causes of war are craving, ill-will and ignorance. Only in developing paññā can we eliminate craving, ill-will and ignorance.

The eightfold Path leads to nibbāna. Nibbāna is the end of all defilements. It can be realized here and now, in this life. When paññā has been developed stage by stage it can reach the degree that enlightenment can be attained. At that moment nibbāna is experienced[1]. When one has realized nibbāna one understands what it means to be "awakened to the truth".

---

[1] Paññā which experiences the nāmas and rūpas of our life is "mundane" or "lokiya paññā"; paññā which experiences nibbāna is "supramundane" or "lokuttara paññā".

Chapter 3

The Teaching of Dhamma

The Buddha proved his compassion for men in his teaching of Dhamma. One may wonder why it is especially the teaching of Dhamma that proves the Buddha's compassion. Are there no other ways of helping people, such as visiting the sick and speaking kind words to other people in order to make them happy? It is true that one can help one's fellow men in doing good deeds and in speaking kind words. However, it is not possible to give them true happiness in this way. When one is kind to other people one might help them in so far as one can make them feel more relaxed or less depressed for a moment. However, there are people who tend to go on being anxious and depressed, no matter how kindly one treats them.

The Buddha knew that the deepest cause of happiness and sorrow is within man. It is not possible to give other people real happiness; one can only be a condition for them to feel happy for a while. The Buddha helped people in the most effective way: he helped them to have right understanding about their life, about themselves, and about the way to find true happiness.

His disciples followed his example and helped people by teaching them Dhamma. We read in the *Discourse on an Exhortation to Channa* (Middle Length Sayings III, no. 144) that Sāriputta and Mahā Cunda, while they were staying on Mount Vulture Peak, visited a sick monk whose name was Channa. First Sāriputta asked Channa how he was feeling, and then he offered to give him the right kind of food and medicines, and to attend personally to his needs if he wanted this. However, he knew that kind words and deeds were not enough. When it was the right moment Sāriputta and Mahā Cunda spoke to Channa about the Dhamma, in order to help him to have right understanding about his life.

In the *Discourse on the Analysis of the Undefiled* (Middle Length Sayings III, no. 139) we read that the Buddha, when he was staying near Sāvatthī in the Jeta Grove, spoke about the eightfold

Path which is the "Middle Way". One should not be intent on the happiness of sense-pleasures and on the other hand not be intent on the practice of self-mortification. The Buddha told his disciples that they should not say of other people that they are walking the right path or the wrong path; he said that there should be neither approval nor disapproval of persons, but that they should teach them what is the right course and what is the wrong course. They should teach them which cause brings which effect. They should simply teach Dhamma. Dhamma means everything that is real. The Buddha helped people to develop right understanding about everything one can experience, no matter whether it is good or bad.

If one wants to eliminate defilements one should first understand what are akusala cittas and what are kusala cittas and be aware of them when they arise. Only when we can be aware of cittas when they appear will we know them as they are. We will not know cittas by speculation. As we have seen, cittas do not last. Citta arises and then falls away immediately to be followed by the next citta. There is only one citta at a time. Life consists of an unbroken series of cittas, arising and falling away continuously. There is no moment without citta. There are many kinds of cittas which perform different functions such as seeing, hearing and thinking. Moreover, there are akusala cittas, unwholesome cittas, and kusala cittas, wholesome cittas. An akusala citta and a kusala citta cannot arise at the same moment since there can be only one citta at a time. However, akusala cittas may arise shortly after kusala cittas have fallen away, even during the time one is doing a good deed. When the kusala cittas have fallen away, regret about one's good deed may arise. This is akusala.

In the *Discourse on an Exhortation to Channa* mentioned above, we read that Channa suffered severe pains. As he could not stand the pains any longer he committed suicide. The Buddha knew that before the moment of his death Channa had kusala cittas after the akusala cittas which motivated him to perform this unwholesome deed. He was able to purify himself of defilements after his deed. The Buddha said therefore: "He took the knife to himself without incurring blame". We do not know about the citta of someone else from the outward appearance of his deeds, because we do not know each different moment of citta. We can only find out with regard to ourselves at which moment there is akusala citta or kusala citta, and even that is most difficult.

Akusala cittas can be rooted in three different unwholesome "roots", "akusala hetus". They are:

attachment (in Pāli: lobha)
aversion or *ill-will* (in Pāli: dosa)
ignorance (in Pāli: moha)

By the word "root" is meant the foundation of the citta. The root is the foundation of the citta just as the root of a tree supports the tree and makes it grow. There are many different degrees of these three akusala hetus.

All akusala cittas are caused by moha, ignorance. Ignorance is, for example, not knowing what is unwholesome and what is wholesome, and not knowing which cause brings which result in life. There are many degrees of moha. An animal has a great deal of moha; it does not know about kusala and akusala, it does not know how to cultivate wholesomeness. However, not only animals have moha, human beings can have a great deal of moha as well. Akusala cittas arise more often than kusala cittas and thus there are countless moments of moha, no matter whether we are walking, standing, sitting or lying down. Moha can only be completely eradicated when paññā has been developed to the degree that one can reach perfection, that is, when one has become an arahat at the attainment of the fourth and last stage of enlightenment[1].

When the citta which arises is accompanied by lobha, attachment, and by moha, the citta is called "lobha-mūla-citta", or citta rooted in attachment[2]. At that moment there is not only moha, which is common to all akusala cittas but there is lobha as well. Lobha-mūla-citta which has moha and lobha as roots is different from the citta which is rooted only in moha, ignorance of realities. Lobha can be greed, lust, selfish desire, and it can be a very subtle form of attachment as well, a form of attachment one can hardly recognize if one does not yet have the right understanding.

Lobha can be accompanied by pleasant feeling. For instance,

---

[1] There are four stages of enlightenment and at each stage defilements are progressively eradicated.

[2] Mūla means root; it is the same as hetu.

when we enjoy beautiful music there is lobha-mūla-citta. Then the citta is akusala, although this kind of lobha is not as gross as greed or lust. One might be inclined to think that whenever there is pleasant feeling, the citta which is accompanied by this feeling must be kusala citta. However, when there is pleasant feeling the citta is not necessarily kusala citta; pleasant feeling can also accompany akusala citta. For instance, when we do a good deed there can be kusala citta with pleasant feeling, but when we feel happy because of beautiful music or a beautiful view, the citta is akusala; it is lobha-mūla-citta with pleasant feeling. We can be deluded about the truth very easily. We find feeling so important that we cannot see anything else. We are unable to know whether the citta is akusala or kusala because we pay attention only to the feeling at that moment.

Lobha-mūla-cittas, cittas rooted in attachment, can be accompanied either by pleasant feeling or by indifferent feeling. When we want to do something such as standing up, walking, taking hold of an object, the lobha-mūla-cittas which arise may be accompanied by indifferent feeling. We do not, usually, have pleasant feeling when we stand up or when we reach for a glass of water. We cannot help having lobha very often. All people, except arahats are bound to have lobha.

The Buddha did not speak to those who still have defilements in terms of "sin" or "punishment". The Buddha pointed out everything which is real and he explained which cause would bring which effect. The bad deeds one does will bring about their own results, just as a seed produces a tree. This is the law of cause and result, of "kamma" and "vipāka". The Buddha explained to his disciples that there should be neither approval nor disapproval of persons, but that they should simply teach Dhamma. In that way people will know what is real. Lobha is real and one should therefore know what lobha is, what its characteristic is, and when it arises.

Another unwholesome root is dosa, aversion. When the citta which arises is accompanied by dosa and moha, the citta is called "dosa-mūla-citta", citta rooted in aversion. At that moment there is not only moha, which is common to all akusala cittas, but there is dosa as well. Dosa appears in its coarsest form as anger or ill-will. There is dosa when one hurts or kills a living being, when one speaks harsh words, or when one curses. Dosa is always accompanied by unpleasant feeling.

There are more subtle forms of dosa as well: dosa can be a slight aversion when we see or hear something unpleasant, or when we are in a bad mood. Dosa can be recognized by the feeling which accompanies it. Even when there is a very vague feeling of uneasiness we can be sure there is dosa. Dosa arises quite often in a day. We are bound to have dosa when there is a loud noise or an ugly sight.

There are three "wholesome roots" or "sobhana hetus", which are the opposite of the akusala hetus. They are:

non-attachment (alobha)
non-aversion or kindness (adosa)
wisdom (amoha or paññā)

Kusala cittas are not accompanied by lobha, dosa or moha. They are always accompanied by alobha, non-attachment, and adosa, non-aversion, but not always by paññā. Thus, citta can be kusala without wisdom (paññā). One can, for example, help other people without understanding that helping is kusala and that wholesome deeds bring pleasant results. However, when there is paññā the citta has a higher degree of wholesomeness. If one observes the precepts[1] only because one considers them as rules, prescribed in the teachings, without any understanding of the reasons for those precepts, ill deeds can be suppressed, but not at all times. If the temptations are too strong one will transgress the precepts. If one has understanding of unwholesome deeds and wholesome deeds, and knows the effect of those deeds, this understanding is a condition for observing the precepts more often. We can develop more wholesomeness in understanding realities, in understanding their causes and effects.

Everyone, except the arahat, has both akusala cittas and kusala cittas. Each citta arises because of the appropriate conditions. Cittas cannot arise without conditions. It depends on various conditions whether there will be akusala citta or kusala citta. We all

[1] Laypeople can observe five precepts, which are rules of training to abstain from killing, stealing, sexual misconduct, lying and the taking of intoxicants, including alcoholic drinks.

have accumulated conditions for both unwholesomeness and wholesomeness. If the present citta is akusala one accumulates a condition for more unwholesomeness and if the present citta is kusala one accumulates a condition for more wholesomeness. For example, when we have a slight feeling of aversion, there is dosa-mūla-citta. If dosa-mūla-cittas occur quite often, we accumulate dosa and dosa becomes a habit. If one is easily inclined to strong dosa it can motivate unwholesome deeds and unwholesome speech.

One may wonder how one can accumulate unwholesomeness and wholesomeness, as each citta which arises falls away completely. Each citta which arises falls away completely but it conditions the succeeding citta. Cittas arise and fall away in succession. That is the reason why past accumulations can go on from one moment to the next moment. If we understand how different people's accumulations are we will be less inclined to blame other people when they do wrong. We will try to help them to have right understanding of the accumulation of kusala and akusala. If we have more right understanding of the conditions which make us act the way we do we will be able to lead a more wholesome life.

One may wonder what the Buddha taught about the will or intention which motivates ill deeds and good deeds. Is there no "free will" which can direct one's actions, speech and thinking? When we think of a "free will", we generally think of a "self" who has control over one's decisions to do good or to do wrong. However, cittas arise because of their own conditions; there is no "self" who can let cittas arise at will.

The Pāli term "kamma" literally means action. In reality kamma is intention or volition. It is not that which is generally understood by "free will". Kamma does not last, it arises and falls away with the citta. Thus, one should not take it for "self" or as belonging to a "self". Kusala kamma or akusala kamma is volition which motivates good or bad deeds. For example, there is akusala kamma through the body when one hits someone; there is akusala kamma through speech when one speaks harsh words or when one curses someone; there is akusala kamma through the mind when one has the intention to take away something which belongs to someone else, or when one plans to kill someone.

The Buddha taught that everyone will experience the result of the kamma he has performed; one will reap what one has sown. Kamma is the cause which produces its result. The mental result of kamma is a type of citta which is called "vipākacitta". Akusala kamma will bring an unpleasant result or akusala vipākacitta; kusala kamma will bring a pleasant result or kusala vipākacitta.

People are born with different mental capacities, with different bodily features and in different circumstances. In the *Discourse on the Lesser Analysis of Deeds*(Middle Length Sayings III, no. 135) we read that, when the Buddha was staying near Sāvatthī in the Jeta Grove, the brahman Subha asked him what the cause was of the differences among human beings:

> *"Now, good Gotama, what is the cause, what is the reason that lowness and excellence are to be seen among human beings while they are in human form? For, good Gotama, human beings of short lifespan are to be seen and those of long lifespan; those of many and those of few illnesses; those who are ugly, those who are beautiful; those who are of little account, those of great account; those who are poor, those who are wealthy; those who are of lowly families, those of high families; those who are weak in wisdom, those who are full of wisdom."*

The Buddha answered Subha:

> *"Deeds (kamma) are one's own, brahman youth, beings are heirs to deeds, deeds are matrix, deeds are kin, deeds are arbiters. Deed divides beings, that is to say by lowness and excellence."*

Not only birth in a certain plane of existence and in certain surroundings is the result of kamma. Throughout our life we receive unpleasant and pleasant results. Everyone would like to experience only pleasant things through eyes, ears, nose, tongue and bodysense. However, everyone is bound to experience both unpleasant and pleasant things through the five senses because everyone has performed both akusala kamma and kusala kamma.

A deed we have performed may produce a result shortly afterwards, or it may produce a result a long time afterwards. We should remember that volition or kamma which motivates a deed is a mental phenomenon and that it can therefore be accumulated. Thus, it can bring about its result later on. The Buddha taught that the akusala kamma and the kusala kamma we have accumulated throughout our life and during countless existences before this life, will produce their results when there are the right conditions for the results to be produced. Vipākacitta is the result of kamma. When we see unpleasant things, there is at that moment akusala vipāka, which is the result of akusala kamma. This akusala vipākacitta receives an unpleasant object through the eyes. When we see pleasant things, the kusala vipākacitta, which is the result of kusala kamma, receives a pleasant object through the eyes. When we hear unpleasant things the akusala vipākacitta, which is the result of akusala kamma, receives an unpleasant object through the ears. When we hear pleasant things the kusala vipākacitta, which is the result of kusala kamma, receives a pleasant object through the ears. There is vipāka every time we see, hear, smell, taste or receive an impression through body-contact. We cannot prevent the arising of vipākacitta; we cannot help seeing, hearing, smelling, tasting and receiving impressions through body-contact. Each citta, and thus also each vipākacitta, has its own conditions; nobody can make cittas arise at will. Which particular vipākacitta arises at the present moment is beyond control. When one does good deeds one can be sure that those deeds will bring a pleasant result, but the moment when the result will take place depends on other conditions as well.

The akusala vipākacitta which experiences an unpleasant object through the eyes, is not the same as the akusala vipākacitta which experiences an unpleasant object through the ears. There is not a "self" who experiences different unpleasant and pleasant objects through the five senses. Each citta has its own conditions and it is different from all other cittas. The more one realizes this truth, the less will one be inclined to believe in a "self".

Vipākacittas arise and fall away within split-seconds, like all other types of citta. After the vipākacittas have fallen away another type of citta arises; for example, a citta which likes or dislikes the object, that is, lobha-mūla-citta or dosa-mūla-citta. If people do not know the different types of cittas, they may be inclined to think that like or dislike is still vipāka. However, like and dislike arise after the vipākacittas have fallen away; they are not the result of kamma. Lobha-mūla-citta or dosa-mūla-citta is not vipākacitta but akusala citta.

Different types of citta succeed one another very rapidly. For example, when we hear a harsh sound, the vipākacitta arises at the moment the sound is perceived through the ears and then falls away immediately. The moments of vipāka are extremely short. After that there may be akusala cittas. For instance, dislike of the sound may arise, and this follows so closely that it seems to occur at the same moment as the hearing. In reality these cittas do not arise at the same moment. Each citta has its own conditions and each citta performs its own function. Vipākacitta is the result of former akusala kamma or kusala kamma. The like or dislike after the vipāka is unwholesome. We should realize that through the arising of akusala citta more akusala is accumulated and that this leads to still more unwholesomeness in our lives.

Many times we may not know at which moment there is vipāka and at which moment there is akusala citta, because we find our feelings about the object we experience so important. The pleasant feeling which accompanies lobha-mūla-citta and the unpleasant feeling which accompanies dosa-mūla-citta can be so strong that we are carried away by these feelings. Thus we cannot see things as they are.

Part of our life is spent in receiving pleasant or unpleasant results and part of our life is spent with akusala cittas or kusala cittas which can motivate unwholesome or wholesome deeds. These deeds condition life in the future, they condition the results which will be received in the future. If we have more understanding of vipāka, which is the result of our own deeds, it will help us to be more patient when there are unpleasant results in our life. We will not blame other people for unpleasant vipāka we receive, because kamma is the real cause of vipāka. We will give in less to our feelings concerning vipāka when we know the different cittas which arise at different moments.

Indeed, the Buddha showed his great compassion in teaching people to understand reality, in teaching them Dhamma.

Chapter 4

Wholesome Deeds

The Buddha helped people to have right understanding of unwholesomeness and wholesomeness; he helped them by teaching them Dhamma. Dhamma excels all other gifts, because the most beneficial gift one can give others is helping them to develop right understanding so that they can lead a more wholesome life. In this way they will find more happiness.

In the *Gradual Sayings* (Book of the Twos, Ch IV, § 2) we read that it is not easy to repay one's parents for all they have done:

> *Monks, it is not an easy task to repay two persons, I declare*[1]*. What two? Mother and father. Even if one should carry about his mother on one shoulder and his father on the other, and so doing should live a hundred years, attain a hundred years; and if he should support them, anointing them with unguents... if he should establish his parents in supreme authority, in the absolute rule over this mighty earth abounding in the seven treasures–not even thus could he repay his parents. What is the cause of that? Monks, parents do much for their children: they bring them up, they nourish them, they introduce them to this world.*
>
> *Moreover, monks, whoso incites his unbelieving parents, settles and establishes them in faith; whoso incites his immoral parents, settles and establishes them in morality; whoso incites his stingy parents, settles and establishes them in liberality; whoso incites his foolish parents*[2]*, settles and establishes them in wisdom,— such a one, just by so doing, does repay, does more than repay what is due to his parents.*

In this sutta the Buddha points out how important it is to help other people to have right understanding about the development of wholesomeness; he explained that this is the way to repay

[1] The English translation has: one can never repay... Here I followed the Thai translation.

[2] who have little understanding

one's parents. Establishing one's parents in faith is mentioned first. The word "faith" however, is not used in the sense of "faith in a person". The Buddha did not want people to perform wholesome deeds in obedience to him or in obedience to certain rules. Faith means confidence in wholesomeness, confidence that the cultivation of wholesomeness is beneficial. Therefore, any time there is wholesomeness there must be faith. After faith the above-quoted sutta speaks about "morality", and then generosity is mentioned. Wisdom or right understanding is mentioned last.

When the different ways of kusala kamma are explained in the suttas, dāna or generosity is usually mentioned first, sīla or morality is mentioned next, and after that "bhāvanā" or mental development. There are many ways to develop kusala and understanding of these ways conditions the performing of them. Paññā, understanding, is the factor which above all conditions the elimination of akusala and the development of kusala. There can be dāna and sīla without paññā, but when there is paññā, dāna and sīla are of a higher degree of kusala. There can be no bhāvanā or mental development without paññā. Paññā is an indispensable factor for bhāvanā, and on the other hand paññā is developed through bhāvanā.

Paññā, understanding things as they are, will help people to lead a more wholesome life. There are many levels of paññā. To the extent that paññā is developed defilements will be eliminated and thus people will find peace of mind. It is beneficial to develop right understanding of akusala as akusala and of kusala as kusala and to help others to develop this understanding as well.

All akusala cittas are caused by ignorance or moha. There are different types of akusala citta. Some akusala cittas are rooted in moha alone. There are also akusala cittas rooted in moha and lobha. Lobha is attachment, selfishness or greed. Furthermore there are akusala cittas rooted in moha and dosa. Dosa is aversion, ill-will or anger. Unwholesome deeds are motivated by akusala cittas.

When there is kusala citta there are no lobha, dosa or moha with the citta. Wholesome deeds are motivated by kusala cittas. When we perform dāna, sīla or bhāvanā, there are no lobha, dosa or moha with the kusala cittas which motivate these wholesome deeds. It is helpful to know more about dāna, sīla and bhāvana in order to lead a more wholesome life.

One way of developing wholesomeness is dāna. Dāna is giving useful things to other people, for example, giving away food, clothing or money to those who are in need. True generosity is a way of eliminating defilements: at such moments we think of other people, we have no selfish thoughts. When there is generosity there are no lobha, dosa or moha.

Giving with the right understanding that generosity is kusala is more wholesome than giving without this understanding. People who give with the understanding that this wholesome act is a means to have less selfishness, are stimulated to develop more wholesomeness. One may think it a selfish attitude to consider one's own accumulation of kusala. However, it is not a selfish attitude. When we have the right understanding of the ways to develop kusala, it is the condition for kusala cittas to arise more often and this is to the benefit of everyone. It is to our fellow-man's advantage too when lobha, dosa and moha are eliminated. It is more agreeable to live with someone who is not selfish and who is not angry than with a selfish or an angry person.

There are many degrees of paññā. When paññā is more highly developed, one understands that it is not "self" who performs wholesome deeds, but cittas which are conditioned by the accumulation of kusala in the past. Thus there is no reason for conceit or pride. By the development of paññā, which is a mental phenomenon and which is not "self", more wholesomeness can be accumulated.

Young children in Thailand are trained to give food to the monks and thus they accumulate kusala. The Thais call the performing of good deeds "tham bun". When children learn to do good deeds at an early age it is a condition for them to continue to be generous when they are grown-up.

When someone gives food to the monks, it is the giver in the first place who will benefit from this wholesome act; the monks give him the opportunity to develop wholesomeness. The monks do not thank people for their gifts; they say words of blessing which show that they rejoice in the good deeds of the giver. One might find it strange at first that the monks do not thank people, but when there is more understanding of the way wholesomeness is developed, one sees these customs in another light.

Even when we are not giving something away ourselves, there is still opportunity to develop wholesomeness in appreciating the good deeds of other people: at that moment there are no lobha, dosa or moha. The appreciation of other people's good deeds is a way of kusala kamma included in dāna as well. It is to everyone's advantage when people appreciate one another's good deeds. It contributes to harmonious living in society.

The third way of kusala kamma included in dāna concerns giving others, no matter whether they are in this world or in other planes of existence, the opportunity to appreciate our good deeds so that they can have kusala cittas as well. In performing kusala we can help others to perform kusala as well. It is very inspiring to see other people looking after their old parents, or to see people studying and teaching Dhamma. We should follow the example of the Buddha. We should continually think of means to help others to develop wholesomeness. This way of kusala kamma is a means to eliminate our defilements. There are opportunities to develop kusala at any moment. When we have developed more wisdom we will try not to waste the opportunity for kusala which presents itself, because human life is very short.

There are three ways of kusala kamma included in sīla or morality. The first way is observing the precepts. Laypeople usually observe five precepts. These precepts are:

abstaining from killing living beings
abstaining from stealing
abstaining from sexual misbehaviour
abstaining from lying
abstaining from the taking of intoxicants
including alcoholic drinks

One can observe these precepts just because one follows the rules without thinking about the reason why one should observe them. Observing them is kusala kamma, but the degree of wholesomeness is not very high if there is no right understanding. One observes the precepts with paññā when one understands that one purifies oneself of akusala while one observes them.

The killing of a living being is akusala kamma. One may wonder whether it is not sometimes necessary to kill. Should one not kill when there is a war, should one not kill insects to protect the crops, should one not kill mosquitos to protect one's health? The Buddha knew that so long as people were living in this world they would have many reasons for transgressing the precepts. He knew that it is very difficult to observe all the precepts and that one cannot learn in one day to observe them all. Through right understanding, however, one can gradually learn to observe them. The precepts are not worded in terms of, for example, "You shall not kill". They are not worded as commandments, but they are worded as follows: "I undertake the rule of training to refrain from destroying life."

The Buddha pointed out what is unwholesome and what is wholesome, so that people would find the way to true peace. It is Paññā or right understanding which will lead people to train themselves in the precepts. Without paññā they will transgress them very easily when the temptations are too strong, or when the situation is such as to make it very difficult for people to observe them. When paññā is more developed it conditions the observing of the precepts more often. One will find out from experience that the precepts are transgressed because of lobha, dosa and moha. When it has been understood that observing the precepts is a way of eliminating defilements, one will even refrain from intentionally killing mosquitos and ants. We always accumulate dosa when there is the intention to kill, even if it is a very small insect. We should find out for ourselves that we accumulate akusala when killing living beings, no matter whether they are human beings or animals. However, we cannot force others to refrain from killing living beings.

To refrain from killing is a kind of dāna as well–it is the gift of life, one of the greatest gifts we can give. The classification of kusala kamma as to whether it be dāna or sīla is not very rigid. The way realities are classified depends on their different aspects.

As regards the taking of intoxicants, people should find out for themselves how much unwholesomeness is accumulated in this way. Even if one has but a slight attachment to them, one accumulates unwholesomeness, and this may be harmful in the future. When the attachment is strong enough it will appear in one's speech and deeds. Even the taking of a little amount of an alcoholic drink can cause one to have more greed, anger and ignorance. It may have the effect that people do not realize what they are doing and that they cannot be aware of the realities of the present moment. Paññā will induce one to drink less and less and eventually to stop drinking. One does not have to force oneself not to drink, one just loses the taste for alcohol because one sees the disadvantages of it. In this way it becomes one's nature not to drink. The person who has developed paññā to such degree that he attains the first stage of enlightenment, the "streamwinner" or "sotāpanna", will never transgress the five precepts again; it has become his nature to observe them.

The second way of kusala kamma included in sīla is paying respect to those who deserve respect. It is not necessary to show respect according to a particular culture; the esteem we feel for someone else is more important. This induces us to have a humble attitude towards the person who deserves respect. The way in which people show respect depends on the customs of the country where they are living or on the habits they have accumulated. In Thailand people show respect to monks, teachers and elderly people in a way different from the way people in western countries show their respect. In some countries the respect people feel towards others may appear only in a very polite way of addressing them.

Politeness which comes from one's heart is kusala kamma; at that moment there are no lobha, dosa and moha. It is kusala kamma to show respect to monks, to teachers and to elderly people. In Thailand people show respect to their ancestors; they express their gratefulness for the good qualities of their ancestors. This is kusala kamma. It is not important whether ancestors are able to see the people paying respect to them or not. We cannot know in which plane they have been reborn–in this human plane, or in some other plane of existence where they might be able to see people paying respect to them. It is wholesome to think of one's ancestors with gratefulness.

We should always try to find out whether there are akusala cittas or kusala cittas which motivate a deed, in order to understand the meaning of that deed. Thus we will understand and appreciate many customs of the Thais and we will not so easily misjudge them or find them superstitious. In the same way we should understand the paying of respect to the Buddha image. It is not idol worship; indeed, it is kusala kamma if one thinks of the Buddha's excellent qualities: of his wisdom, of his purity and of his compassion. One does not pray to a Buddha in heaven, because the Buddha does not stay in heaven or in any plane of existence; he passed away completely. It is wholesome to be grateful to the Buddha and to try to follow the Path he discovered. In which way one shows respect to the Buddha depends on the inclinations one has accumulated.

The third way of kusala kamma included in sīla is helping other people by words or deeds. The act of helping other people will have a higher degree of wholesomeness if there is the right understanding that helping is kusala kamma, and that this is a way to eliminate selfishness and other defilements. Thus one will be urged to perform more kusala kamma; one will be more firmly established in sīla. It is therefore more wholesome to perform sīla with right understanding or paññā.

Performing one's duties is not always kusala kamma: people may perform their duties just because they are paid for their work. For example, a teacher teaches his pupils and a doctor takes care of his patients because it is their profession to do so. However, they can develop wholesomeness if they perform their duties with kindness and compassion.

Paññā conditions one to perform kusala kamma, no matter what one's duties are. Wholesomeness can be developed at any time we are with other people, when we talk to them or listen to them.

Helping other people with kind words and deeds alone is not enough. When it is the right moment we can help others in a deeper and more effective way, that is, helping them to understand who they are, why they are in this world and what the aim of their life in this world is. This way of helping is included in bhāvanā or mental development.

Chapter 5

Mental Development

The Buddha said that one should realize the impermanence of all things. Everybody is subject to old age, sickness and death. All things are susceptible to change. What one is enjoying today may be changed tomorrow. Many people do not want to face this truth; they are too attached to the pleasant things they can enjoy through eyes, ears, nose, tongue and bodysense. They do not realize that these things are not true happiness.

The Buddha cured people's ignorance by helping them to have right understanding about their life; he taught them Dhamma. The Buddha taught different ways of developing wholesomeness: dāna or generosity, sīla or morality and bhāvanā or mental development. Bhāvanā is a way of kusala kamma which is on a higher level, because wisdom is developed through bhāvanā.

One may wonder why wisdom, paññā, is essential. The answer is that only understanding things as they are can eliminate ignorance. Out of ignorance people take what is unwholesome for wholesome. Ignorance causes sorrow. The Buddha always helped people to have right understanding of their different cittas. He explained what akusala cittas and kusala cittas are, in order that people could develop more wholesomeness.

We can verify in our life that the Buddha taught the truth. His teachings are true not only for Buddhists, but for everybody, no matter what race or nationality he is or what religion he professes. Attachment or greed (in Pāli: lobha), aversion or anger (in Pāli: dosa) and ignorance (in Pāli: moha) are common to everybody, not only to Buddhists. Should not everyone eradicate lobha, dosa and moha?

People do not always realize that lobha, dosa and moha lead to sorrow. They may recognize unwholesomeness when it is coarse, but not when it is more subtle. For example, they may know that the citta is unwholesome when there is lobha which is as coarse as greed or lust, but they do not recognize lobha when it is more subtle, such as attachment to beautiful things or to dear people. Why is it unwholesome to have attachment to our relatives and friends? It is true that we are bound to have lobha, but we should realize that attachment is not the same as pure loving-kindness (in Pāli: mettā). When we think that we have pure loving-kindness, there can be moments of attachment too. Attachment is not wholesome; it will sooner or later bring unhappiness. Although people may not like to see this truth, one day they will experience that lobha brings unhappiness. Through death we are bound to lose people who are dear to us. And when sickness or old age affect our sense faculties we may no longer be able to enjoy beautiful things through eyes and ears.

If we do not have the right understanding of the realities of life we will not know how to bear the loss of dear people. We read in the *Udāna* (Verses of Uplift, Ch VIII, Pāṭaligāma, §8, Khuddaka Nikāya) that, while the Buddha was staying near Sāvatthī in East Park, at the storeyed house of Migāra's mother, Visākhā came to see him. Visākhā who had lost her grand-daughter came to see the Buddha with wet clothes and wet hair. The Buddha said:

"Why, Visākhā! How is it that you come here with clothes and hair still wet at an unseasonable hour?"

"O, sir, my dear and lovely grand-daughter is dead! That is why I come here with hair and clothes still wet at an unseasonable hour."

"Visākhā, would you like to have as many sons and grandsons as there are men in Sāvatthī?"

"Yes, sir, I would indeed!"

"But how many men do you suppose die daily in Sāvatthī?"

"Ten, sir, or maybe nine, or eight. Maybe seven, six, five or four, three, two; may be one a day dies in Sāvatthī, sir. Sāvatthī is never free from men dying, sir."

"What think you, Visākhā? In such case would you ever be without wet hair and clothes?"

"Surely not, sir! Enough for me, sir, of so many sons and grandsons!"

"Visākhā, whoso have a hundred things beloved, they have a hundred sorrows. Whoso have ninety, eighty... thirty, twenty things beloved... whoso have ten... whoso have but one thing beloved, have but one sorrow. Whoso have no thing beloved, they have no sorrow. Sorrowless are they and passionless. Serene are they, I declare."

People who see that it is unwholesome to be enslaved by attachment to people and to the things around themselves, want to develop more understanding of realities by applying themselves to bhāvanā, mental development. Studying the Buddha's teachings and explaining them to others is kusala kamma included in bhāvanā. In studying the teachings paññā will be developed. If we want to understand what the Buddha taught it is essential to read the scriptures as they have come down to us at the present time in the "Three Collections": the "Vinaya", the "Suttanta" and the "Abhidhamma". Study alone, however, is not enough. We should experience the truth of Dhamma in daily life. Only then will we know things as they really are. Teaching Dhamma to other people is kusala kamma of a high degree. In this way one not only helps others to have more understanding about their life, one develops one's own understanding as well. Teaching Dhamma is the most effective way of helping other people to develop kusala and to eradicate akusala.

Another way of kusala kamma included in bhāvanā is the development of calm or "samatha bhāvanā". In samatha there are specific meditation subjects which can condition the calm which is temporary freedom from lobha, dosa and moha. One must have right understanding of the meditation subject and of the way to become calm. When samatha has been highly developed different stages of jhāna or absorption can be attained. However, the attainment of jhāna is extremely difficult and one must have accumulated the right conditions in order to attain it. When the citta is jhānacitta there are no lobha, dosa and moha. Jhāna is kusala kamma of a high degree. Jhāna is not the same as a trance which might be experienced after taking certain drugs. Those who take drugs want to obtain the desired end in an easy way and their action is prompted by lobha. Those who apply themselves to samatha have the sincere wish to purify themselves of lobha, dosa and moha; they do not look for sensational or thrilling experiences.

Samatha can purify the mind, but it cannot eradicate unwholesome latent tendencies. When the citta is not jhānacitta, lobha, dosa and moha are bound to arise again. The person who applies himself to samatha cannot eradicate the belief in a self, and so long as there is the concept of self, defilements cannot be eradicated.

The clinging to the concept of self can only be eradicated through vipassanā. Vipassanā or "insight meditation" is another way of kusala kamma included in bhāvanā. Through the development of vipassanā ignorance of realities is eliminated. One learns to see things as they are in being aware, for example, when one sees, hears, smells, tastes, when one receives impressions through the bodysense or when one thinks. When we experience that all things in ourselves and around ourselves are only mental phenomena or nāma and physical phenomena or rūpa which arise and fall away, we will be less inclined to take them for self.

What is the reason that we all are inclined to cling to a self? The reason is that because of our ignorance we do not know things as they really are. When we hear a sound, we are ignorant of the different phenomena which occur during the moment we are hearing that sound. We think that it is a self who is hearing. However, it is not a self who is hearing; it is a citta which hears the sound. Citta is a mental phenomenon, it is nāma, that is, the reality which experiences something. The citta which hears experiences sound. Sound itself does not experience anything, it is rūpa. Rūpa is the reality which does not experience anything. Sound and earsense are conditions for hearing. Earsense is rūpa as well. One may wonder whether it is true that earsense does not experience anything. Earsense is a kind of rūpa in the ear which has the capacity to receive sound, but it does not experience the sound. It is only a condition for the nāma which experiences the sound. Each citta has its own conditions through which it arises. Seeing is conditioned by eyesense which is rūpa and by visible object which is also rūpa. There is no self who performs different functions such as seeing, hearing, smelling, tasting, receiving impressions through the bodysense and thinking. These are different nāmas, each of which arises because of its own conditions.

We read in the *Greater Discourse on the Destruction of Craving* (Middle Length Sayings I, no. 38) that the Buddha, while he was staying near Sāvatthī, in the Jeta Grove, spoke to the monk Sāti who had a misconception about the Buddha's teachings. Sāti understood from the Buddha's teachings that consciousness lasts, and that it is one and the same consciousness which speaks, feels, and experiences the results of good and bad deeds. Several monks heard about Sāti's wrong view. After they had tried in vain to dissuade him from his wrong view, they spoke to the Buddha about him. The Buddha summoned Sāti and said to him:

"Is it true, as is said, that a pernicious view like this has accrued to you, Sāti: 'In so far as I understand Dhamma taught by the Lord, it is that this consciousness itself runs on, fares on, not another'?"

"Even so do I, Lord, understand Dhamma taught by the Lord: it is this consciousness itself that runs on, fares on, not another."

"What is this consciousness, Sāti?"

"It is this, Lord, that speaks, that feels, that experiences now here, now there, the fruition of deeds that are lovely and that are depraved."

"But to whom, foolish man, do you understand that Dhamma was taught by me thus? Foolish man, has not consciousness generated by conditions been spoken of in many a figure by me, saying: 'Apart from condition there is no origination of consciousness'? But now you, foolish man, not only misrepresent me because of your own wrong grasp, but you also injure yourself and give rise to much demerit which, foolish man, will be for your woe and sorrow for a long time."

... Then the Lord addressed the monks, saying:

"Do you, monks, understand that Dhamma was taught by me thus so that this monk Sāti, a fisherman's son, because of his own wrong grasp not only misrepresents me but is also injuring himself and giving rise to much demerit?"

"No, Lord. For in many a figure has consciousness generated by conditions been spoken of to us by the Lord, saying: 'Apart from condition there is no origination of consciousness.' "

"It is good, monks, it is good that you understand thus Dhamma taught by me to you, monks. For in many a figure has consciousness generated by conditions been spoken of by me to you, monks, saying: 'Apart from condition there is no origination of consciousness.'

... It is because, monks, an appropriate condition arises that consciousness is known by this or that name: if consciousness arises because of eye and material shapes, it is known as seeing-consciousness; if consciousness arises because of ear and sounds it is known as hearing-consciousness; if consciousness arises because of nose and smells, it is known as smelling-consciousness; if consciousness arises because of tongue and tastes it is known as tasting-consciousness; if consciousness arises because of body and touches, it is known as tactile-consciousness; if consciousness arises because of mind and mental objects, it is known as mental consciousness. Monks, as a fire burns because of this or that

> *appropriate condition, by that it is known; if a fire burns because of sticks, it is known as a stick-fire; and if a fire burns because of chips, it is known as a chip-fire; and if a fire burns because of grass, it is known as a grass-fire; and if a fire burns because of cowdung, it is known as a cowdung-fire; and if a fire burns because of chaff, it is known as a chaff-fire; and if a fire burns because of rubbish, it is known as a rubbish-fire. Even so, monks, when because of a condition appropriate to it consciousness arises, it is known by this or that name...* "

Thinking about different kinds of nāma and rūpa and the conditions for their arising will help us to have right understanding of them. However, this is not the same as the direct experience of the truth. We will understand what nāma and rūpa really are when we know through direct experience their different characteristics as they appear one at a time through eyes, ears, nose, tongue, bodysense and mind.

Nāma and rūpa arise and fall away so rapidly that we do not realize that there are different nāma-units and different rūpa-units. For example, only perceiving sound is a moment which is different from liking or disliking the sound. We are often inclined to find our like or our dislike with regard to the object we experience so important that we do not notice the characteristic of the nāma or rūpa which appears at that moment. Thus we cannot see things as they are; we take like or dislike for self. Like and dislike are only nāmas arising because of conditions; like and dislike are due to one's accumulations. There are conditions for each citta; there is no self who can let any citta arise at this or at that moment.

We do not only take mental phenomena for self, we take the body for self as well. However, the body consists of nothing else but different rūpa-elements which arise and fall away. There are many different kinds of rūpa. The rūpas which can be directly experienced through the bodysense are: hardness or softness, heat, cold, motion and pressure. These rūpas can be directly experienced through the bodysense, there is no need to think about them or to name them. The direct understanding of rūpas whenever they appear is the only way to know that they are different rūpas and that we should not take them for self.

Different characteristics of nāma and rūpa can be known one at a time as they appear through the five sense-doors and through the mind-door. So long as we do not know them as they are we are bound to take them for self. We are not used to being aware of the phenomena of our life; for example, we are not used to being aware of seeing. Seeing is a nāma which experiences only what appears through the eyesense, that is, visible object. This type of nāma is real and thus it can be experienced. Before one thinks about what one has seen, there must be the experience of what appears through the eyes, of visible object. We are used to paying attention only to the thing or the person we think about after there has been seeing and thus we are ignorant of the nāma which only experiences visible object, the nāma which sees. The nāma which sees is different from the types of nāma which like or dislike the object or which think about it. If one does not know seeing as it is, one is bound to take it for self. It is the same with hearing, which is just the perceiving of sound. When hearing arises we can learn to be aware of its characteristic; it can be known that it is nāma, a reality which just perceives sound through the ears. We can gradually become familiar with the characteristic of hearing and then we will know that it is different from thinking and from other types of nāma. We will learn that it is different from rūpa. Thus we will be less inclined to take it for self.

We can be aware of only one characteristic of nāma or rūpa at a time. For example, when we hear, there are both hearing and sound, but we cannot be aware of hearing and sound at the same time, since each citta experiences only one object at a time. There can be awareness of sound at one moment and of hearing at another moment, and thus we will gradually learn that their characteristics are different.

Only if we learn to be aware of the nāma or rūpa which appears at the present moment will we see things as they are. Thinking about nāma and rūpa, reminding ourselves of them or naming realities "nāma" and "rūpa" is still not the direct experience of reality. If we only think of nāma and rūpa and do not learn to experience their characteristics, we will continue to cling to them and we will not become detached from the idea of self. It is beyond control which characteristic presents itself at a particular moment. We cannot change the reality which has appeared already. We should not think that there should be awareness of hearing first and after that of thinking about what we heard. Different realities will appear at different moments and there is no particular sequence we should follow when we are mindful of realities.

In the beginning we are not able to know the arising and falling away of nāma and rūpa through direct experience. We should just learn to be aware of whatever characteristic of nāma or rūpa presents itself. When, for example, smelling appears, we cannot help smelling. At that moment we can learn to be aware of the characteristic of smelling, without making any special effort. There is no need to think about it or to remind ourselves that it is smelling, or that it is nāma.

It is essential to realize that awareness[1] is a type of nāma as well, which can only arise when there are the right conditions. There is no self who is aware or who can let awareness arise at will. Right understanding of the development of vipassanā is a condition for the arising of awareness. After a moment of awareness there will be a long time without awareness, or there will be moments when we are only thinking about nāma and rūpa. In the beginning there cannot be a great deal of awareness, but even a short moment of right awareness is beneficial, because paññā developed through the direct experience of realities is of a higher degree than the paññā developed through thinking about realities or the paññā developed in samatha. Vipassanā is kusala kamma of a very high degree, because vipassanā leads to detachment from the concept of self and eventually to the eradication of all defilements. If there is less lobha, dosa and moha, it is for the happiness of the whole world as well.

In the *Gradual Sayings* (Book of the Nines, Ch II, § 10, Velāma) we read that the Buddha, while he was dwelling near Sāvatthī, at Jeta Grove, in Anāthapiṇḍika's Park, spoke to Anāthapiṇḍika about different degrees of wholesome deeds which bring their fruits accordingly. Giving gifts to the Buddha and the Order of monks, and taking one's refuge in the Buddha, the Dhamma and the Sangha are deeds which are of a high degree of kusala, but there are other ways of kusala which are of still higher degrees.

---

[1] Awareness or mindfulness is in Pāli: sati. It is a mental factor which accompanies each sobhana citta, "beautiful citta". Sati is heedful, non-forgetful of what is wholesome. There are different levels of sati: there is sati with dāna, with sīla, with samatha and with vipassanā. Sati in vipassanā is aware, mindful, non-forgetful of the characteristic of nāma or rūpa which presents itself through one of the six doors. Further on in this book I will explain more about sati.

We read that the Buddha said:

> *... though with pious heart he took refuge in the Buddha, the Dhamma and the Sangha, greater would have been the fruit thereof, had he with pious heart undertaken to keep the precepts: abstention from taking life, from taking what is not given, from carnal lusts, from lying and from intoxicating liquor, the cause of sloth.*
>
> *...though with pious heart he undertook to keep these precepts, greater would have been the fruit thereof, had he made become a mere passing fragrance of loving-kindness.*
>
> *...though he made become just the fragrance of loving-kindness, greater would have been the fruit thereof, had he made become, just for a finger-snap, the perception of impermanence.*

The perception of impermanence is developed when there is a moment of right awareness of nāma or rūpa. One may be surprised that the perception of impermanence is more fruitful than other kinds of wholesome deeds. It is right understanding which realizes the impermanence of nāma and rūpa and this kind of understanding can change our life. It can eventually eradicate our clinging, aversion and ignorance. The time will come when we have to leave this world because of old age, sickness or accident. Is it not better to take leave of the world with understanding of what things are than to part from the world with aversion and fear?

Chapter 6

The Buddha

In the Buddhist temples of Thailand we see people paying respect in front of the Buddha statue by kneeling and touching the floor three times with their hands and head. Those who have just arrived in Thailand may wonder whether this way of paying respect is a form of prayer or whether it has another meaning. Buddhists in Thailand express in this way their confidence in the "Three Gems": the Buddha, the Dhamma and the Sangha. They take their refuge in the "Three Gems".

The first Gem is the Buddha. When people take their refuge in the Buddha, they say the following words in Pāli: "Buddhaṃ saraṇaṃ gacchāmi", which means, "I go for refuge to the Buddha". What is the meaning of the word "Buddha"? The *Illustrator of Ultimate Meaning* (the "Paramatthajotikā", a commentary to the "Minor Readings", Khuddaka Nikāya) explains, in the commentary to the "Three Refuges", the meaning of the word "Buddha":

> *... and this is said, "Buddha": in what sense buddha? He is the discoverer (bujjhitā) of the Truths, thus he is enlightened (buddha). He is the enlightener (bodhetā) of the generation, thus he is enlightened. He is enlightened by omniscience, enlightened by seeing all, enlightened without being led by others... he is quite without defilement, thus he is enlightened; he has travelled by the Path that goes in only one way, thus he is enlightened; he alone discovered the peerless complete enlightenment, thus he is enlightened; ... Buddha: this is not a name made by a mother, made by a father... this (name) "Buddha", which signifies final liberation, is a realistic description of Enlightened Ones, Blessed Ones, together with their obtainment of omniscient knowledge at the root of an enlightenment (tree).*

The Buddha is the discoverer of the truth. What is the truth the Buddha discovered all by himself? "He is enlightened by omniscience, enlightened by seeing all..." the commentary to the

Paramatthajotikā says. He had developed the wisdom to see and to experience the truth of all things. Everything in life is impermanent and thus it is unsatisfactory. People suffer from old age, sickness and death. In spite of this truth people still cling to the things in and around themselves. Thus they are not able to see reality. The Buddha understood through direct experience that all phenomena which arise fall away immediately. He did not cling to anything at all.

For us it is difficult to experience the truth of impermanence. Nāma and rūpa arise and fall away all the time, but one cannot have direct understanding of impermanence if one's wisdom is not developed. It is difficult to be aware often of realities when they appear and to realize what they are: only nāma and rūpa, phenomena which are impermanent and not self. The more we realize how difficult it is to see things as they are, the more we understand that the Buddha's wisdom must have been of the highest degree.

The Buddha taught that everything in life is dukkha. Dukkha literally means pain, misery or suffering. However, the experience of the truth of dukkha is much deeper than a feeling of sorrow or contemplation about suffering. It is the direct understanding of the impermanence of the nāmas and rūpas in our life and the realization that none of these phenomena is true happiness. Some people may think that pondering over this truth is already the experience of the truth of dukkha. However, one does not have the real understanding of the truth if one merely thinks about it. When paññā has been developed to the degree that the arising and falling away of nāma and rūpa are directly understood, one will come to realize the truth of dukkha. Then one will gradually learn to be less attached to nāma and rūpa.

In the *Greater Discourse of a Full Moon*(Middle Length Sayings III, no. 109) we read that the Buddha, while he was staying near Sāvatthī, in the palace of Migāra's mother, in the Eastern Monastery, asked the monks:

> *"What do you think about this, monks? Is material shape permanent or impermanent?"*
>
> *"Impermanent, revered sir."*
>
> *"But is what is impermanent painful or is it pleasant?"*

> *"Painful, revered sir."*
>
> *"And is it right to regard that which is impermanent, suffering, liable to change, as, 'This is mine, this am I, this is myself?"*
>
> *"No, revered sir."*

The Buddha asked the same question about mental phenomena.

Everything in our life is impermanent. Also what we call happiness is impermanent–it is only a mental phenomenon which arises and then falls away immediately. How can that which arises and falls away as soon as it has arisen be real happiness? Everything in life, even happiness, is therefore dukkha or unsatisfactory. What arises and falls away should not be taken for self; everything is anattā or "non-self". Impermanence, dukkha and anattā are three aspects of the truth, the truth of all realities within ourselves and around ourselves. It may take us a long time before we can experience things as they really are. The only way to develop direct understanding of the truth is being aware of the nāma and rūpa which appear, such as, for example, seeing, hearing or thinking at this moment.

The Buddha was always mindful and clearly conscious. He did not have ignorance of any reality. When we realize how difficult mindfulness is we deeply respect the great wisdom of the Buddha. The Buddha is called the "Awakened One", because he is awakened to the truth. We read in the *Discourse with Sela* (Middle Length Sayings II, no. 92) that the Buddha said to Sela:

> *"What is to be known is known by me, and to be developed is developed, what is to be got rid of has been got rid of–therefore, brahman, am I awake."*

The Buddha had, by his enlightenment, attained the greatest purity. He had completely eradicated all defilements. The Buddha attained enlightenment during his life in this world. He taught others to develop in their daily lives the wisdom which can completely eradicate defilements and all latent tendencies. The more we know about our own defilements, including the more subtle defilements, and the more we see how deeply rooted the clinging to the concept of self is, the more will we realize the high degree of the Buddha's purity.

The Buddha was full of compassion for everybody. The fact that the Buddha was free from defilements did not mean that he wanted to dissociate himself from the world. On the contrary, he wanted to help all beings who still had defilements to find the Path leading to true understanding. People are inclined to think that Buddhism makes people neglectful of their duties towards others and that it makes them self-centered. This is not so. Buddhism enables one more fully to perform one's duties and to serve other people in a more unselfish way.

The Buddha attained enlightenment for the happiness of the world. In the *Gradual Sayings* (Book of the Ones, Ch XIII) we read that the Buddha said to the monks:

> *Monks, there is one person whose birth into the world is for the welfare of many folk, for the happiness of many folk; who is born out of compassion for the world, for the profit, welfare and happiness of devas and mankind. Who is that one person? It is a Tathāgata*[1] *who is arahat, a fully Enlightened One. This, monks, is that one person.*

The more one understands the Buddha's teachings, the more one is impressed by his compassion for everybody. The Buddha knew what it meant to be free from all sorrow. Therefore he helped other beings to attain this freedom as well. One can help people by kindness, by generosity, and in many other ways. The most precious thing one can give others is to show them the way to true peace. The Buddha proved his great compassion to people by teaching them Dhamma.

When Buddhists pay respect to the Buddha statue they do not pray to a Buddha in heaven, since the Buddha passed away completely. Buddhists pay respect to the Buddha statue because they think with deep reverence and gratefulness of the Buddha's virtues: of his wisdom, his purity and his compassion. When we speak of virtues we think of good qualities in someone's character. There are many degrees of good qualities however. When the wisdom of him who follows the eightfold Path is developed to such an extent that he can attain enlightenment, then his way of life will have become purer and his compassion for others deeper. Wisdom

[1] Literally, "thus gone", the Perfect One.

is not only theoretical knowledge of the truth, but realizing the truth in one's life as well. The virtues of the Buddha were developed to such degree that he not only attained enlightenment without the help of a teacher, but was also able to teach the truth to others, so that by following the right Path they could attain enlightenment.

There were other Buddhas before the Buddha Gotama. All Buddhas find the truth by themselves, without being led by others. However, there are two different kinds of Buddhas: the "Sammāsambuddha", that is, a "Universal Buddha" or "Perfectly Enlightened One"[1], and the "Pacceka Buddha" or "Silent Buddha". The Sammāsambuddha has found the truth and is able to teach others as well the way to enlightenment. The Pacceka Buddha has not accumulated virtues to the same extent as the Sammāsambuddha and thus he is not as qualified in teaching others as the Sammāsambuddha. The Buddha Gotama was a Sammāsambuddha. There cannot be more than one Sammāsambuddha in a Buddha era; neither can there be in that era Pacceka Buddhas. The Buddha era in which we are living will be terminated when the Buddha's teachings have disappeared completely. The Buddha foretold that the further one is away from the time he lived, the more his teaching will be misinterpreted and corrupted. His teachings will disappear completely and then there will be a next Buddha, and so the next Buddha era. The next Buddha will discover the truth again and he will teach other beings the way to enlightenment.

Buddhists take their refuge in the Buddha. What does the word "refuge" mean? The *Paramatthajotikā commentary* speaks about the meaning of the word "refuge":

> *... When people have gone for refuge, then by that very going for refuge it combats, dispels, carries off, and stops their fear, anguish, suffering, (risk of) unhappy destination (on rebirth), and defilement... The going for refuge is the arising of cognizance with confidence therein and giving preponderance thereto, from which defilement is eliminated and eradicated, and which occurs in the mode of taking that as the highest value...*

[1] Sammā means thoroughly, rightly.

Going for refuge to the Buddha does not mean that the Buddha can eradicate people's defilements. We read in the *Mahā-Parinibbāna-sutta* (Dialogues of the Buddha II, no. 73) that, before his passing away, the Buddha said to Ānanda:

> *Now I am frail, Ānanda, old, aged, far gone in years. This is my eightieth year and my life is spent... Therefore, Ānanda, be an island to yourself, a refuge to yourself, seeking no external refuge; with Dhamma as your island, Dhamma as your refuge, seeking no other refuge.*

The Buddha then explained that one takes one's refuge in the Dhamma by developing the "four Applications of Mindfulness", that is, being mindful of nāma and rūpa in order to develop right understanding of them. This is the eightfold Path which leads to enlightenment. One can depend only on oneself in following this Path, not on anyone else.

The Buddha said that the Dhamma and the Vinaya would be his successor. Today the Buddha is no longer with us, but we take our refuge in the Buddha when we have confidence in his teachings and we consider it the most important thing in life to practise what he taught.

Chapter 7

The Dhamma

The second of the Three Gems Buddhists take their refuge in is the Dhamma. When they take their refuge in the Dhamma they say: "Dhammaṃ saraṇaṃ gacchāmi", which means, "I go for refuge to the Dhamma."

What does the word "dhamma" mean? Most people think that dhamma only means doctrine, but the word "dhamma" has several more meanings. Dhamma means everything which is real, no matter whether it is good or bad. Dhamma comprises, for example, seeing, sound, greed and honesty. We cannot take our refuge in every dhamma; for instance we cannot take our refuge in greed or hate.

Can we take refuge in our good deeds? The effect of a good deed is never lost, since each good deed will bring its fruit accordingly. In the *Kindred Sayings* (I, Sagāthā-vagga, Ch I, part 8, Slaughter Suttas, § 5) we read that a deva (divine being) asks the Buddha how a man should live so that he does not have to fear life in another world. The Buddha answered:

Let him but rightly set both speech and mind.
And by the body work no evil things.
If in a house well stored with goods he dwell,
Let him have faith[1]*, be gentle, share his goods*
With others, and be affable of speech.
In these four qualities if he persist,
He need not fear life in another world.

A good deed can cause a happy rebirth such as birth in the human plane of existence, or in a heavenly plane, and in that case one need not fear life in another world. However, even a heavenly plane is not a permanent refuge. Life in a heavenly plane may last very long, but it is not permanent. There may be

[1] Confidence in wholesomeness.

rebirth in unhappy planes after one's lifespan in a happy plane is terminated, depending on which of one's accumulated good and bad deeds, kusala kamma and akusala kamma, will produce result[1]. Each deed will bring its own result: a wholesome deed will bring a pleasant result and an unwholesome deed will bring an unpleasant result. Some deeds may produce a result in this life, other deeds may produce result in a future life. The accumulated unwholesome and wholesome deeds may cause births in different planes of existence at different times. In the *Kindred Sayings* (I, Sagāthā-vagga, Ch III, Kosala, Part 2, § 10, Childless) we read about someone who gave alms to a Pacceka Buddha. Because of this good deed he was reborn in heaven seven times and after that in the human plane, which is also kusala vipāka. However, he killed his nephew because he wanted his brother's fortune. This ill deed caused him to be reborn in hell. Thus he received the results of kusala kamma and of akusala kamma at different times.

So long as all defilements and latent tendencies have not been eradicated, there will be rebirth in different planes of existence. Even those who are reborn in heavenly planes still have defilements and latent tendencies. Birth is sorrow, no matter in what plane; birth will be followed by death. We read in the *Kindred Sayings* (II, Nidāna-vagga, Ch XV, part 1, § 3, Tears) that the Buddha, while he was in the Jeta Grove, near Sāvatthī, said to the monks:

> *Incalculable is the beginning, monks, of this faring on. The earliest point is not revealed of the running on, faring on, of beings cloaked in ignorance, tied to craving.*
>
> *As to that, what do you think, monks? Which is greater,— the flood of tears shed by you crying and weeping as you fare on, run on this long while, united as you have been with the undesirable, separated as you have been from the desirable, or the waters in the four seas?*
>
> *... For many a long day, monks, have you experienced the death of mother, of son, of daughter, have you experienced the ruin of kinsfolk, of wealth, the calamity of disease. Greater is the flood of tears shed by you*

[1] Kamma is volition, but the terms kusala kamma and akusala kamma stand also for good action or evil action motivated by wholesome or unwholesome volition. Deeds bring their results accordingly; more precisely: the volition or intention which motivates a deed is accumulated and can produce result later on.

> *crying and weeping over one and all of these, as you fare on, run on this many a long day, united with the undesirable, separated from the desirable, than are the waters in the four seas.*

Only when all defilements have been eradicated will there be no cause any more which can produce a next life; that is the end of rebirth , and that means the end of all sorrow. Nibbāna is the end of rebirth because nibbāna is the end of defilements[1] . Therefore one can truly take one's refuge in nibbāna. In the suttas, nibbāna is called "the deathless". We read in the *Kindred Sayings* (V, Mahā-vagga, Book I, Kindred Sayings on the Way, I, Ignorance, § 7) that, when the Buddha was at Sāvatthī, a monk said to him:

> *" 'The deathless! The deathless!', lord, is the saying. Pray, lord, what is the deathless, and what the way to the deathless?"*
>
> *"That which is the destruction of greed, the destruction of hatred, the destruction of ignorance, monk–that is called 'the deathless'. This same ariyan eightfold way is the way to the deathless."*

Nibbāna is the dhamma we can take our refuge in, nibbāna is included in the second Gem. Nibbāna is a Gem of the highest value, because there is nothing to be preferred to complete freedom from all sorrow, from birth, old age and death. Nibbāna is real. If one has not yet attained enlightenment, one has not experienced nibbāna. But if one follows the right Path one may realize nibbāna, even during this life.

Nibbāna is the deathless, it is the end of the cycle of birth and death. People may think that is not very desirable not to be born again. It does not make much sense to speculate about nibbāna; if we have not attained enlightenment we cannot imagine what nibbāna is like. At the present time we can experience our defilements; we can experience the sorrow which is caused in the world by greed, hatred and ignorance. We read in the *Kindred Sayings* (I, Sagāthā-vagga, Ch III, Kosala, Part 3, § 3, the World)

[1] There are four stages of enlightenment. At each of these stages nibbāna is experienced and defilements are progressively eradicated. Only when the last stage of enlightenment, the stage of the arahat, has been attained, there is the end of defilements and there will be the end of rebirth. This will be further explained in Ch. 8.

that, when the Buddha was at Sāvatthī, King Pasenadi asked him:

> *"How many kinds of things, Lord, that happen in the world, make for trouble, for suffering, for distress?"*
> *"Three things, sire, happen of that nature.*
> *What are the three?*
> *Greed, hatred and ignorance:— these three make for trouble, for suffering, for distress."*

Who does not want to be free from suffering, caused by greed hatred and ignorance? Those who want to become free from all defilements take refuge in nibbāna. What is the Path leading to nibbāna? Nibbāna cannot be attained merely by wishing for it. Can people attain nibbāna by doing good deeds? Even when one performs good deeds there can still be the idea of self. When one does good deeds but there is no development of right understanding of realities, the belief in a self and other defilements cannot be eradicated. Thus, good deeds alone, without right understanding, cannot lead to nibbāna. Only vipassanā can lead to the attainment of nibbāna, to the eradication of defilements.

On may wonder whether it is necessary, in addition to developing vipassanā, to do other good deeds. There is no self who can choose to perform a particular kind of kusala. The Buddha encouraged us to perform all kinds of kusala for which there is an opportunity. Sometimes there is an opportunity for dāna, sometimes for sīla, at other times for samatha or for vipassanā. Through the development of vipassanā we will come to know our defilements, even the more subtle ones. Then we will see the danger of defilements more clearly and realize the benefit of developing the Path leading to their eradication. If we observe the precepts or do other kinds of good deeds with mindfulness of nāma and rūpa, we will learn that there is no self who performs kusala and thus kusala will be purer. However, vipassanā will not immediately transform one's character. It is most important to develop right understanding of both kusala and akusala as only conditioned realities, as non-self.

The development of vipassanā takes many lives, because ignorance is deeply accumulated. Most of the time we are ignorant and forgetful of the nāma and rūpa which appear now through one of the five senses or through the mind-door. We are used to thinking of realities which have fallen away already a long time ago or of those which may present themselves in the future. We should not expect to learn awareness in one day or even within one year. We cannot tell how much progress is made each day, because wisdom develops very gradually.

We read in the *Kindred Sayings* (III, Khandhā-vagga, Middle Fifty, Part 5, § 101, Adze-handle) that the Buddha, when he was at Sāvatthī, said to the monks:

> *By knowing, monks, by seeing is, I declare, the destruction of the āsavas*[1]*, not by not knowing, by not seeing...*
>
> *Suppose, monks, in a monk who lives neglectful of self-training there should arise this wish: "O that my heart were freed from the āsavas without grasping." Yet for all that his heart is not freed from the āsavas. What is the cause of that?*
>
> *It must be said that it is his neglect of self-training. Self-training in what? In the four applications of mindfulness... in the ariyan eightfold Path.*
>
> *... in the monk who dwells attentive to self-training there would not arise such a wish as this: "O that my heart were freed from the āsavas without grasping"; and yet his heart is freed from them. What is the cause of that?*
>
> *It must be said it is his attention to self-training... Just as if, monks, when a carpenter or carpenter's apprentice looks upon his adze-handle and sees thereon his thumb-mark and his finger-marks he does not thereby know: "So and so much of my adze-handle has been worn away today, so much yesterday, so much at other times." But he knows the wearing away of it just by its wearing away.*
>
> *Even so monks, the monk who dwells attentive to self-training has not this knowledge: "So and so much of the āsavas has been worn away today, so much yesterday, so much at other times." But he knows the wearing away of them just by their wearing away.*

When wisdom is highly developed, nibbāna can be realized. There are four stages of enlightenment and at each stage nibbāna is experienced and defilements are progressively eradicated.

[1] Cankers or intoxicants, one group of defilements. Defilements are classified into different groups.

Defilements are so deeply rooted that they can only be eradicated stage by stage. At the first stage the wrong view of self is eradicated, but there are still attachment, aversion and ignorance. Only at the last stage of enlightenment, the stage of the arahat, are all defilements and latent tendencies eradicated completely. When one has attained the stage of the arahat there will be no more rebirth.

The citta which experiences nibbāna is a "supramundane" or lokuttara citta. There are two types of citta for each of the four stages of enlightenment: lokuttara kusala citta and its result, the "fruition-consciousness"; thus there are eight types of lokuttara citta. Nibbāna and the eight types of lokuttara citta which experience nibbāna are included in the second Gem, the Dhamma to which one goes for refuge[1]. When we take our refuge in the second Gem, we consider it the goal of our life to develop the wisdom which can eventually eradicate all defilements.

There is still another Dhamma included in the second Gem, namely the Dhamma in the sense of the Buddha's teachings. We can take our refuge in the Buddha's teachings. The teachings can lead people to the truth if they study them with right understanding and if they practise according to what is taught. We should study the whole of the Buddha's teachings. If one studies only a few suttas one will not clearly understand what the Buddha taught. Many times a sutta merely alludes to things which are explained in detail in other parts of the Tipiṭaka, the "three Collections" of the scriptures. It is useful to study the commentaries to the Tipiṭaka as well, because they explain the Buddha's teachings. The teachings are our guide since the Buddha passed away.

We read in the *Discourse to Gopaka-Moggallāna*(Middle Length Sayings III, no. 108) that after the Buddha's passing away a brahman asked Ānanda what the cause was of the unity of the monks. He said:

> *"Is there, good Ānanda, even one monk who was designated by the good Gotāma, saying: 'After my passing this one will be your support', and to whom you might have recourse now?"*
>
> *"There is not even one monk, brahman, who was designated by the*

[1] Nibbāna and the eight lokuttara cittas are the "nine supramundane dhammas", "nava lokuttara dhammas".

Lord who knew and saw, perfected one, fully Self-Awakened One, saying: 'After my passing this one will be your support', and to whom we might have recourse now."

"But is there even one monk, Ānanda, who is agreed upon by the Order and designated by a number of monks who are elders, saying: 'After the Lord's passing this one will be our support', and to whom you might have recourse now?"

"There is not even one monk, brahman, who is agreed upon by the Order... and to whom we might have recourse now."

"But as you are thus without support, good Ānanda, what is the cause of your unity?"

"We brahman, are not without support, we have a support, brahman. Dhamma is the support."

In the *Gradual Sayings*(Book of the Threes, Ch VI, § 60, Sangārava) we read that the Buddha spoke to the brahman Sangārava about three kinds of "marvels": the marvel of "superpower", such as diving into the earth or walking on water, the marvel of thought-reading and the marvel of teaching. The Buddha asked him which marvel appealed to him most. Sangārava answered:

Of these marvels, master Gotama, the marvel of super-power... seems to me of the nature of an illusion. Then again as to the marvel of thought-reading... this also, master Gotama, seems to me of the nature of an illusion. But as to the marvel of teaching... of these three marvels this one appeals to me as the more wonderful and excellent.

The teachings are the greatest miracle because they can change a person's life. Through the Dhamma one is able to follow the Path which eventually leads to the end of all sorrow, to the end of the cycle of birth and death. The Buddha's teachings do not appeal to everyone. Many people find it difficult to think in a way which is different from the way they used to think. They do not like the truth of non-self. They want to be master of their mind even though they can find out that this is impossible. The Buddha knew how difficult it is for people to change their way of thinking. In the *Discourse to Vacchagotta on Fire*(Middle Length Sayings II, no. 72) we read that the Buddha, when he was staying near Sāvatthī, in the Jeta Grove, taught Dhamma to Vacchagotta who had wrong views. Vacchagotta, after having brought forward his wrong views and having listened to the Buddha's reply, said that he was at a loss and bewildered on account of what the Buddha had said to him. The Buddha replied:

> *You ought to be at a loss, Vaccha, you ought to be bewildered. For, Vaccha, this dhamma is deep, difficult to see, difficult to understand, peaceful, excellent, beyond dialectic, subtle, intelligible to the wise; but it is hard for you who are of another view, another allegiance, another objective, of a different observance, and under a different teacher.*

Dhamma is deep and difficult to understand. People cannot understand Dhamma if they still cling to their own views. If they would really study the teachings and apply what they have learnt, they could find out for themselves whether one can take one's refuge in the Dhamma. When we have verified in our life that what the Buddha taught is reality, even if we cannot yet experience everything he taught, we do not want to exchange our understanding for anything else in life. If we develop right understanding of realities we will have Dhamma as a support. Thus we take refuge in the Dhamma.

Chapter 8

The Sangha

The Sangha is the third of the "Three Gems". When Buddhists take their refuge in the Sangha they say: "Saṅghaṃ saraṇaṃ gacchāmi", which means, "I go for refuge to the Sangha". The word "sangha" literally means "congregation" or "community". It is the word generally used for the order of monks. However, the word "sangha" in connection with the third Gem has a different meaning. The third Gem, the Sangha we take our refuge in, is the "ariyan Sangha", the community of all those who have attained enlightenment. "Ariyan" or "noble person" is the name which denotes all those who have attained one of the four stages of enlightenment, no matter whether they are monks, nuns (bhikkhunīs), unmarried layfollowers or married layfollowers. In the suttas we read that countless men and women layfollowers, single and married, attained enlightenment[1].

In order to understand what enlightenment is, we should first know more about the accumulation of defilements. All kinds of defilements which arise are conditioned; they are conditioned by akusala in the past. Akusala citta which arises now conditions akusala citta again in the future. Each citta which arises falls away completely and thus we may wonder how there can be accumulation of defilements. Each citta which arises falls away but it conditions the succeeding citta and this again the next one. Since our life is a continuous series of cittas succeeding one another, the process of accumulation continues in this series of cittas, going on from moment to moment, from birth to death, and from one life to the next life. That is the reason why there are conditions at present for all kinds of defilements; they can arise at any time when there are the right conditions.

The defilements which have been accumulated are very deeply rooted, and they can only be eradicated in stages, at the different

[1] See, for example, Middle Length Sayings II, no. 73, "Greater Discourse to Vacchagotta".

stages of enlightenment. First the latent tendency of the clinging to the concept of self has to be eradicated. The belief in a self can be eradicated by understanding what it is we take for self, in developing vipassanā or right understanding of realities. What we call "my body" are only physical phenomena, rūpas, which arise and fall away and which we cannot control. We read in the *Kindred Sayings* (III, Middle Fifty I, § 59, The Five) that the Buddha said to his first five disciples in the Deerpark of Vārānasi:

> *Body, monks, is not the self. If body, monks, were the self, then body would not be involved in sickness, and one could say of body: "Thus let my body be. Thus let my body not be."*

The same is said about mental phenomena. What we take for "my mind" are only mental phenomena, nāmas, which arise and fall away and which are beyond control. There is no self who can direct them. The wrong view of self we have accumulated throughout countless lives can be eliminated only very gradually. The wisdom becomes keener as successive stages of insight are attained during the development of vipassanā. When the first stage of enlightenment is attained and nibbāna is experienced for the first time, the wrong view of self is eradicated completely and there is no more doubt about nāma and rūpa.

The first stage of enlightenment is the stage of the "streamwinner", in Pāli: "sotāpanna". We read in the *Kindred Sayings* (III, Khandhavagga, Ch XXV, Kindred Sayings on Entering, § 1, The Eye) that the Buddha said to the monks:

> *The eye, monks, is impermanent, changeable, becoming otherwise. The ear, monks, is impermanent, changeable. So is the nose, the tongue, the body, and the mind. It is impermanent, changeable, becoming otherwise...*
>
> *He, monks, who thus knows, thus sees these doctrines, is called "streamwinner, saved from destruction, assured, bound for enlightenment".*

The sotāpanna, the streamwinner, is bound for the last stage of enlightenment, which is the stage of the arahat. At the first stage of enlightenment, the stage of the sotāpanna, nibbāna is experienced and defilements are eradicated, but not all defilements are eradicated yet. There are still lobha, dosa and moha. The sotāpanna knows that there are still conditions for akusala cittas, but he does not take them for self. Although he still has defilements, he will never transgress the five precepts; it has become his nature to observe them. He cannot commit a deed which can cause rebirth in one of the woeful planes; he is "saved from destruction" as we read in the above-quoted sutta. Those who are not ariyans cannot be sure that they will not be reborn in a woeful plane of existence, even if they have done many good deeds in this life. One may have committed an evil deed in a past life which may cause rebirth in an unhappy plane. Only ariyans can be sure that they will not be reborn in an unhappy plane.

The sotāpanna has an unshakable confidence in the "Three Gems": in the Buddha, the Dhamma and the Sangha. He has no doubts about the Path the Buddha taught; he cannot delude himself about the right practice of vipassanā. We are deluded about the right practice so long as we cling to a self, when we want to induce the arising of awareness or when we cling to results we are hoping for. The sotāpanna, however, is firmly established on the Path to the last stage of enlightenment, the stage of the arahat.

In the scriptures nibbāna has been described as the end of lobha, dosa and moha, as the end of dukkha, as the end of rebirth, as the deathless. When one reads this one may think that the attainment of enlightenment and the experience of nibbāna only pertains to the arahat who has realized the fourth and last stage of enlightenment and who will not be reborn after he has passed away. However, at each of the four stages of enlightenment nibbāna is experienced and defilements are eradicated, until they are all eradicated at the last stage of enlightenment. The ariyans who have not reached the stage of the arahat still have defilements and they still have conditions to be reborn, but they are sure to reach the end of defilements and the end of rebirth.

The sotāpanna has experienced nibbāna. It is difficult to understand and define what nibbāna is. Nibbāna is the unconditioned dhamma, it does not arise and fall away. All realities we experience in daily life arise because of conditions and then fall away immediately. What arises and falls away is dukkha, suffering or unsatisfactory. All conditioned realities are impermanent, dukkha and anattā, non-self. Since nibbāna does not arise and fall away it is not impermanent and thus not dukkha. Nibbāna is not a person or self, it is anattā. Thus, all realities, including nibbāna, are anattā. When paññā has been developed to the degree that conditioned realities are clearly understood as they are, as impermanent, dukkha and anattā, there can be enlightenment, the experience of nibbāna. Nibbāna is the object of lokuttara citta, supramundane citta, as we have seen in chapter 7. The lokuttara cittas which experience nibbāna arise and then fall away immediately, they are impermanent. After they have fallen away other types of cittas arise which are not lokuttara cittas. So long as one has not eradicated all defilements akusala cittas are bound to arise again.

The fact that the sotāpanna has attained enlightenment does not mean that he cannot continue all his daily activities. The sotāpanna can live with husband or wife and lead a family life. Ariyans who have not attained the third stage of enlightenment, the stage of the "non-returner" or "anāgāmī", still have attachment to sense objects. As regards the arahat, he has no inclinations at all for the layman's life.

The sotāpanna does not take any nāma or rūpa for self, but there is still attachment, aversion and ignorance; he still has conceit. Therefore, he has to continue with the development of vipassanā. We read in the *Kindred Sayings* (III, Khandhā-vagga, Last Fifty, II, § 122, Virtue) that Mahā-Koṭṭhita asked Sāriputta what would be the object of awareness for a virtuous monk who has not realized any stage of enlightenment yet, or for a sotāpanna, or for those who have realized the subsequent stages of enlightenment. Sāriputta explained that the object of paññā is the five "khandhas of grasping"[1], which are all the nāmas and rūpas in and around oneself. Sāriputta said:

> *"The five khandhas of grasping, friend Koṭṭhita, are the conditions which should be pondered with method by a virtuous monk, as being impermanent, suffering, sick, as a boil, as a dart, as pain, as ill-health, as alien, as transitory, empty and not self...*

[1] Khandha is translated as "group" or "aggregate". The five khandhas are: the khandha of rūpas, of feelings, of perception, of "formations" or "activities" (all mental factors other than feeling and perception), and of consciousness. Thus, the five khandhas are all nāmas and rūpas of our life.

Indeed, friend, it is possible for a virtuous monk so pondering with method these five khandhas of grasping to realize the fruits of stream-winning."

"But, friend Sāriputta, what are the things which should be pondered with method by a monk who is a sotāpanna?"

"By a monk who is a sotāpanna, friend Koṭṭhita, it is these same five khandhas of grasping which should be so pondered.

Indeed, friend, it is possible for a monk who is a sotāpanna... by so pondering these five khandhas... to realize the fruits of once-returning[1]."

"But, friend Sāriputta, what are the things which should be pondered with method by a monk who is a once-returner?"

"By one who is a once-returner, friend, it is these same five khandhas which should be pondered with method.

Indeed it is possible, friend, for one who is a once-returner, by so pondering to realize the fruits of non-returning[2]."

"But, friend Sāriputta, what are the things which should be pondered with method by one who is a non-returner?"

"By such a one, friend Koṭṭhita, it is these five khandhas of grasping which should be so pondered. It is possible, friend, for a non-returner by so pondering to realize the fruits of arahatship."

"But what, friend Sāriputta, are the things which should be pondered with method by one who is an arahat?"

"By an arahat, friend Koṭṭhita, these five khandhas should be pondered with method as being impermanent, suffering, sick, as a boil, as a dart, as ill-health, as alien, transitory, void and not self.

For the arahat, friend, there is nothing further to be done, nor is there return to upheaping of what is done. Nevertheless, these things, if practised and enlarged, conduce to a happy existence and to self-possession even in this present life."

The ariyan of the second stage, the once-returner or sakadāgāmī, has not eradicated all attachment and aversion, but they have become attenuated. He still has ignorance, which is only completely eradicated by the arahat. The ariyan of the third stage, the non-returner or anāgāmī, has eradicated aversion and he has eradicated

[1] The once-returner or sakadāgāmī has realized the second stage of enlightenment.

[2] The non-returner or anāgāmī has realized the third stage of enlightenment.

attachment to the things experienced through the five senses, but he has not eradicated all forms of clinging; he still clings to rebirth and he still has conceit.

Ariyans who are not yet arahats can still have conceit, although they have no wrong view of self. They may be inclined to pride while they compare themselves with others. When a person thinks himself better than, equal to or less than someone else, there can, even if it is true, be conceit. Why should we compare ourselves with others? In the *Khemaka-sutta* (Kindred Sayings III, Khandhā-vagga, Middle Fifty, Part 4, § 89) we read that the monk Khemaka, who was staying in Jujube Tree Park, was afflicted by sickness. Some other monks who were staying near Kosambī in Ghosita Park, asked the monk Dāsaka to inquire after his health. After he gave the message that his health was not improving, the other monks told Dāsaka to ask Khemaka whether he still took anything for self. When Khemaka had told Dāsaka that he did not take anything for self, the other monks concluded that Khemaka must be an arahat. Khemaka answered Dāsaka:

"Though, friends, I discern in the five khandhas of grasping no self nor anything pertaining to the self, yet am I not arahat, nor one in whom the āsavas (cankers) are destroyed. Though, friend, I see that I have got the idea of 'I am' in the five khandhas of grasping, yet do I not discern that I am this 'I am'."

Then the venerable Dāsaka returned to the monks with that message and reported the words of the venerable Khemaka (and those monks sent this further message): "As to this 'I am', friend Khemaka, of which you speak, what do you mean by this 'I am'? Do you speak of 'I am' as body or as distinct from the body? As feeling, or as distinct from feeling? As perception... as the "activities"... as consciousness, or as distinct from consciousness? As to this 'I am', what do you mean by it?" (So the venerable Dāsaka went again and took the message in these words.)

"Enough, friend Dāsaka. What boots this running to and fro! Fetch my staff. I will go myself to these monks."

So the venerable Khemaka, leaning on his staff, came to those monks. When he got there, he greeted them, and exchanging the courtesies of civil words, sat down at one side. As he thus sat, the elders thus spoke to the venerable Khemaka:—

"As to this 'I am', friend Khemaka, of which you speak, what do you

mean by it? Do you speak of it as body or as distinct from body... as consciousness, or as distinct from consciousness?"

"No friends, I do not say, 'I am body or feeling, or perception, or the 'activities' or consciousness, or as distinct from these and from consciousness.' Though, friends, I see that I have got the idea of 'I am' in the five khandhas of grasping, yet I do not discern that I am this 'I am'. Just as, friends, in the case of the scent of a blue lotus, or a white lotus,— if one should say: 'The scent belongs to the petals or the colour or the fibres of it', would he be rightly describing the scent?"

"Surely not, friend."

"Then how would he be right in describing it?"

"Surely, friend, by speaking of the scent of the flower."

"Even so, friends, I do not speak of the 'I am' as a body, or as feeling and so forth. Nevertheless I see that in these five khandhas of grasping I have got the idea of 'I am'; yet I do not discern that I am this 'I am'. Though, friends, an ariyan disciple has put away the five lower fetters[1]*, yet there remains in him a subtle remnant from among the five khandhas of grasping, a subtle remnant of the I am-conceit, of the I am-desire, of the lurking tendency to think 'I am', still not removed from him. Later on he lives contemplating the rise and fall of the five khandhas of grasping, seeing thus: 'Such is body, such is the arising of body, such is the ceasing of it. Such is feeling... perception... the activities... such is consciousness, the arising of it and the ceasing of it'.*

In this way, as he lives in the contemplation of the five khandhas of grasping, that subtle remnant of the I am-conceit, of the I am-desire, that lurking tendency to think 'I am', which was still not removed from him–that is now removed.

Suppose, friends, there is a dirty, soiled cloth, and the owners give it to a washerman, and he rubs it smooth with salt-earth, or lye or cowdung, and rinses it in pure clean water. Now, though that cloth be clean, utterly cleansed, yet there hangs about it, still unremoved, the smell of the salt-earth or lye or cowdung. The washerman returns it to the owners, and they lay it up in a sweet-scented coffer. Thus that smell... is now utterly removed..."

---

[1] Fetters or saṁyojanas are a group of defilements. The non-returner or anāgāmī has eradicated the five lower fetters, which include wrong views, clinging to sense objects and aversion. The arahat has eradicated the five higher fetters which include conceit, craving for rebirth which is the result of jhāna, restlessness and ignorance.

Further on we read:

> *Now when this teaching was thus expounded the hearts of as many as sixty monks were utterly set free from the āsavas, and so was it also with the heart of the venerable Khemaka.*

The arahat has eradicated all defilements and latent tendencies. He will not be reborn when his life is terminated.

How can we find out who is an ariyan? There is no way to know who is an ariyan, unless we have become enlightened ourselves. It cannot be known from someone's outward appearance whether he is an ariyan or not. People who are very amiable and peaceful are not necessarily ariyans. However, we can take our refuge in the ariyan Sangha even if we do not personally know any ariyans. We can think of the virtues of the ariyans, no matter whether they are in this plane of existence or in other planes. The ariyans prove that there is a way to the end of defilements. We should know what the condition is for the end of defilements: the development of wisdom. The monks, nuns, men and women lay-followers who were ariyans in the Buddha's time proved that what the Buddha taught can be realized in daily life. The Buddha did not teach abstract ideas, he taught reality. Should those who want to realize the truth not walk the same Path the ariyans walked, even if they still have a long way to go?

The ariyans understood very clearly that we cannot seek deliverance from our defilements outside ourselves. Defilements can only be eradicated where they arise: within ourselves. If we want to eradicate defilements we should follow the eightfold Path which is the "Middle Way". In order to follow the "Middle Way" we do not have to change our daily life, we do not have to follow a particular life-style or difficult practices. We can be aware of nāma and rūpa during our daily activities. We will experience that this may be more difficult than the practices of an ascetic. It is harder to overcome the clinging to a self when we are seeing, hearing or thinking, than to endure bodily hardship. The development of wisdom is a lifetask. We need much courage and perseverance in order to continue to be aware of realities of daily life.

When we take our refuge in the ariyan Sangha we are expressing our confidence in the Buddha's Path, through which we may realize what the Sangha has realized. We take our refuge in the Sangha also when we pay respect to the monks, no matter whether they are ariyans or not, because the goal of monkhood is to apply what the Buddha taught in order to realize the truth and to try to help other people as well to realize the truth. Thus the monks remind us of the "Three Gems": the Buddha, the Dhamma and the Sangha.

Chapter 9

Death

It is a reality of life that we are bound to lose those who are dear to us. When a relative or one of our friends dies we feel much grief and we find it difficult to bear our loss. The Buddha's teachings can help us to face reality, to see things as they are. Many times the Buddha spoke about the sorrow caused by the loss of dear people.

We read in the *Discourse on Born of Affection*(Middle Length Sayings II, no. 87):

Thus have I heard: At one time the Lord was staying near Sāvatthī in the Jeta Grove in Anāthapiṇḍika's monastery. Now at that time the dear and beloved little only son of a certain householder had passed away. After he had passed away (the father) had no inclination for work or for food. Going constantly to the cemetery, he wailed: "Where are you, little only son? Where are you, little only son?" Then that householder approached the Lord; having approached, having greeted the Lord, he sat down at a respectful distance. The Lord spoke thus to that householder as he was sitting down at a respectful distance:

"Do you not have, householder, controlling faculties for stilling your own mind? There is a change in your faculties."

"But how could there be no change in my faculties, Lord? For, Lord, my dear and beloved little only son has passed away..."

"That is just it, householder. For, householder, grief, sorrow, suffering, lamentation and despair are born of affection, originate in affection."

"But for whom Lord, could this hold good in this way: 'Grief, sorrow, suffering, lamentation and despair are born of affection, originate in affection'? For, Lord, bliss and happiness are born of affection, originate in affection."

Then the householder, not rejoicing in what the Lord had said, repudiating it, rising from his seat, departed...

The householder could not grasp the deep meaning of the Buddha's words. We should try to understand what the Buddha meant. We should try to understand what the Buddha taught about the world, about ourselves, about life and death. The Buddha summarized his teachings in the "Four Noble Truths".

We read in the *Kindred Sayings* (V, Mahā-vagga, Book XII, Kindred Sayings about the Truths, Ch II, §1) that the Buddha explained the "Four Noble Truths" (ariya sacca) to his first five disciples in the Deerpark in Vārānasi. The first "Noble Truth" is the Truth of "dukkha" which can be translated as suffering or unsatisfactoriness. The Buddha said:

> *Now this, monks, is the ariyan truth about dukkha:*
>
> *Birth is dukkha, decay is dukkha, sickness is dukkha, death is dukkha; likewise sorrow and grief, woe, lamentation and despair. To be conjoined with things we dislike, to be separated from things we like— that also is dukkha. Not to get what one wants–that also is dukkha. In a word, the five khandhas which are based on grasping are dukkha.*

The five khandhas, which are the mental phenomena and the physical phenomena in and around ourselves, are dukkha. One may wonder why they are dukkha. We take the mind for self, but what we call our mind are only mental elements or nāmas which arise and then fall away immediately. We take the body for self, but what we call our body are only physical elements or rūpas which arise and fall away. When we do not know the truth we think that these phenomena can stay; we take them for self. We might for instance think that sadness stays, but there is not only sadness, there are many other phenomena such as seeing, hearing and thinking. What we think is a long time of sadness is, in reality, many different phenomena succeeding one another; none of these phenomena stays.

Phenomena which are impermanent are not real happiness; so they are dukkha. Although dukkha is often translated as "suffering", it is not only an unhappy feeling; the first "Noble Truth" pertains to all phenomena which arise and fall away. There is not anything in our life which is not dukkha. Even happy feeling is dukkha; it does not last.

The second "Noble Truth" is the origin of dukkha, which is craving. The same sutta states:

Now this, monks, is the ariyan truth about the arising of dukkha: It is that craving that leads back to birth, along with the lure and the lust that lingers longingly now here, now there: namely the craving for sensual pleasure, the craving to be born again, the craving for existence to end. Such, monks, is the ariyan truth about the arising of dukkha.

So long as there is craving in any form there will be a condition for life, for the arising of nāma and rūpa. Thus, there will be dukkha.

The third "Noble Truth" is the cessation of dukkha, which is nibbāna. We read in the above quoted sutta:

And this, monks, is the ariyan truth about the ceasing of dukkha:

Verily it is the utter passionless cessation of, the giving up, the forsaking, the release from, the absence of longing for this craving.

Craving is the origin of dukkha, whereas when there is the cessation of craving there will be the extinction of rebirth and thus of dukkha. Nibbāna is the end of dukkha. The arahat has, at the attainment of enlightenment eradicated all craving and thus for him there are no more conditions for rebirth, and that means the end of dukkha[1].

We read in the same sutta about the fourth "Noble Truth":

Now this, monks, is the ariyan truth about the practice that leads to the ceasing of dukkha:

Verily it is the ariyan eightfold way, namely: Right understanding, right thinking, right speech, right action, right livelihood, right effort, right mindfulness, right concentration.

The eightfold Path (ariya-magga) is the development of right understanding of all phenomena which appear in our daily life. We come to know the world in and around ourselves, not through

[1] The ariyans who are not arahats have also at the attainment of enlightenment experienced nibbāna and eradicated defilements, but there are four stages of enlightenment and at these stages defilements are progressively eradicated, as we have seen in Ch 8. The ariyans who are not arahats are sure to reach arahatship. The sotāpanna will not be reborn more than seven times; thus, there is still rebirth for him but he will reach the end of rebirth.

speculation, but from our own experience.

How do we experience the world? We experience the world through seeing, hearing, smelling, tasting, receiving impressions through the bodysense and through the mind. Everything we experience through the doors of the five senses and through the mind-door is extremely short, because all phenomena which arise fall away immediately. When we see, there is the world of visible object, but it does not last, it falls away again. When we hear, there is the world of sound, but it is impermanent. Likewise the world of smell, the world of taste, the world of tangible object and the world of mental objects; none of these worlds lasts.

In the *Visuddhimagga* (VIII, 39) we read about the shortness of the world:

> *...in the ultimate sense the life-moment of living beings is extremely short, being only as much as the occurrence of a single conscious moment. Just as a chariot wheel, when it is rolling, rolls (that is, touches the ground) only on one point of (the circumference of) its tyre, and, when it is at rest, rests only on one point, so too, the life of living beings lasts only for a single conscious moment. When that consciousness has ceased, the being is said to have ceased...*
>
> *Life, person, pleasure, pain–just these alone*
> *Join in one conscious moment that flicks by.*
> *Ceased khandhas of those dead or alive*
> *Are all alike, gone never to return.*
> *No (world is) born if (consciousness is) not*
> *Produced, when that is present, then it lives;*
> *When consciousness dissolves, the world is dead...*

What we call death is not really different from what happens at any moment of consciousness. Each moment a citta falls away there is death of citta. Each citta which arises falls away completely but it conditions the next citta. The last citta of this life, the dying-consciousness (cuti-citta), is succeeded by the first citta of the next life, the rebirth-consciousness (paṭisandhi-citta). There is no self at any moment of our life and thus there is no self or soul which travels from this life to the next life.

It is ignorance which causes us to think and behave as if the body and the mind were permanent. We are attached to the body and to the mind and we take them for self. We think that it is self who sees, hears, thinks and moves around. The clinging to self causes sorrow. We wish to be master of our body and our mind; we wish to control our life and to experience only pleasant things. When we are confronted with old age, sickness and death we are very sad. Those who are ignorant of reality cannot grasp the Buddha's words that sorrow originates in attachment. This is in fact the second "Noble Truth", the truth about the origination of dukkha which is craving. We should realize that all nāmas and rūpas which arise are impermanent, dukkha and anattā (non-self).

The Buddha pointed out the impermanence of phenomena in many different ways. He spoke about the impermanence of the body in order to help people to become detached from the concept of "my body". He spoke about the contemplation of the foulness of the body, and he recommended meditations on corpses in different stages of dissolution. We read in the *Satipaṭṭhāna-sutta* (Middle Length Sayings I, no. 10):

> *And again, monks, as a monk might see a body thrown aside in a cemetary, dead for one day or for two days or for three days, swollen, discoloured, decomposing; he focuses on this body itself*[1], *thinking: "This body, too, is of a similar nature, a similar constitution, it has not got past that (state of things)."*

The *Visuddhimagga* (Ch VI, 88) explains:

> *... For a living body is just as foul as a dead one, only the characteristic of foulness is not evident in a living body, being hidden by adventitious embellishments.*

In order that people might realize the foulness of the living body as well, the Buddha spoke about the "Parts of the Body". We read in the *Satipaṭṭhāna-sutta*:

> *And again, monks, a monk reflects on precisely this body itself, encased in skin and full of various impurities, from the soles of the feet*

[1] His own body.

> *up and from the crown of the head down, that: "There is connected with this body hair of the head, hair of the body, nails, teeth, skin, flesh, sinews, bones, marrow, kidneys, heart, liver, membranes, spleen, lungs, intestines, mesentary, stomach, excrement, bile, phlegm, pus, blood, sweat, fat, tears, serum, saliva, mucus, synovic fluid, urine."*

Reflections on the foulness of the body can help us to become less attached to it, but the most effective way to see the body as it really is, is awareness and direct understanding of the rūpa-elements which constitute the body. We read in the *Satipaṭṭhāna-sutta* that the Buddha spoke about the body in terms of the four elements:

> *And again, monks, a monk reflects on this body according to how it is placed or disposed in respect of the elements, thinking: "In this body there is the element of extension, the element of cohesion, the element of heat, the element of motion."*

The element of extension or solidity (Earth) appears in the characteristics of hardness and softness, the element of cohesion (Water) in the characteristics of fluidity and cohesion, the element of heat (Fire) in the characteristics of heat and cold, the element of motion (Wind) in the characteristics of motion or oscillation and pressure. These elements are the same, no matter whether we experience them in dead matter or in the body. Both dead matter and the body are only elements which are impermanent and non-self.

We should know the world as it really is by experiencing different characteristics of nāma and rūpa when they present themselves through the five sense-doors and through the mind-door. For example, when the characteristic of heat presents itself through the bodysense, it can be object of awareness. When softness appears it can be object of awareness. In this way we will get to know different characteristics of reality through our own experience and we will learn to see them as elements.

It is important to know different characteristics of realities when they present themselves in order to eliminate the clinging to the concept of self. We may think that the softness of the body belongs to "my body". When we learn to be mindful of the characteristic of softness more often we will find out that softness is a characteristic which is the same in dead matter and in the body. We will learn through experience that it is a characteristic which does not know or experience anything; that it is rūpa and not self. Thus we will become less attached to the concept of "my body". When we are aware of realities such as seeing, sadness, happiness and thinking, we will learn that they are only different types of nāma which arise and fall away. They are dukkha. The eye is dukkha, seeing is dukkha, the feelings which arise on account of what is seen are dukkha.

It does not appeal to everybody to be mindful of nāma and rūpa as they appear in daily life. However, we have to consider what we really want in life. Do we want to continue being ignorant and taking body and mind for self? Do we want to live in darkness or do we want to develop wisdom so that there will be an end to dukkha? If we decide that we want to walk the way leading to the end of dukkha, we must develop wisdom in our daily life: when we see, hear or think, when we feel sad and when we feel happy. This is the only way to understand dukkha, the arising of dukkha, the ceasing of dukkha and the way leading to the ceasing of dukkha. When we realize how deeply rooted our ignorance is and how strong the attachment to the self, we will be motivated to learn to be mindful of nāma and rūpa.

The Buddha often spoke about mindfulness of death. He spoke about death in order to remind people of the impermanence of each moment. Life is extremely short and thus we should not waste any time, but we should learn to develop understanding of the present moment so that ignorance of realities can be eliminated.

Ignorance cannot be eradicated within a short time. Only when one has attained the fourth and last stage of enlightenment, the stage of the arahat, are there no more defilements; only then ignorance is completely eradicated. We read in the *Mahā-Parinibbāna-sutta* (Dialogues of the Buddha II, no. 16, Ch VI, 10,11)[1] that when the Buddha passed away those who still had conditions for sorrow wept:

---

[1] I have used the translation of the Wheel Publication no. 67, 68, 69, Buddhist Publication Society, Sri Lanka.

Then, when the Bhagavā[1] *had passed away, some monks, not yet freed from passion, lifted up their arms and wept; and some, flinging themselves on the ground, rolled from side to side and wept, lamenting: "Too soon has the Bhagavā come to his parinibbāna! Too soon has the Happy One come to his parinibbāna! Too soon has the Eye of the World vanished from sight!"*

But the monks who were freed from passion, mindful and clearly comprehending, reflected in this way: "Impermanent are all compounded things. How could this be otherwise?"

And the venerable Anuruddha addressed the monks, saying: "Enough, friends! Do not grieve, do not lament! For has not the Bhagavā declared before, that with all that is dear and beloved there must be change, separation and severance? Of that which has arisen, has come into being, is compounded and subject to decay, how can one say: 'May it not come to dissolution'?"

We read in the same sutta (Ch II, 32) that prior to his passing away the Buddha said to Ānanda:

Now I am frail, Ānanda, old, aged, far gone in years. This is my eightieth year and my life is spent... Therefore, Ānanda, be an island to yourself, a refuge to yourself, seeking no external refuge; with Dhamma as your island, Dhamma as your refuge, seeking no other refuge.

And how, Ānanda, is a monk an island to himself, a refuge to himself, seeking no external refuge; with Dhamma as his island, Dhamma as his refuge, seeking no other refuge?

When he dwells contemplating the body in the body, earnestly, clearly comprehending, and mindfully, after having overcome desire and sorrow in regard to the world; he dwells contemplating feeling in the feelings, mind in the mind, and mental objects in the mental objects, earnestly, clearly comprehending, and mindfully, after having overcome desire and sorrow in regard to the world, then, truly, he is an island to himself, a refuge to himself, seeking no external refuge; having Dhamma as his island and refuge, seeking no other refuge...

---

[1] The Buddha.

When we "contemplate" the body in the body, feeling in the feelings, mind in the mind and mental objects in the mental objects, we will learn not to see the self in the body, feelings, mind and mental objects. Only if we are mindful of all the different kinds of nāma and rūpa which present themselves in our daily life will we see that they are impermanent, dukkha and anattā. This is the only way leading to the end of dukkha, to the end of death.

Chapter 10

Life

What is life? What is the origin of life? How and when does it end? These are questions people keep on asking themselves. Life is nāma and rūpa of the present moment. There is seeing now; is that not life? Attachment, aversion and ignorance may arise on account of what is seen; is that not life? There is thinking of what we have seen, heard, smelt, tasted and touched; is that not life?

We have eyes, ears, nose, tongue, bodysense and mind; we experience objects through these six doorways and on account of what we experience defilements tend to arise. This is life at the present moment. But it was also life in the past and it will be life in the future, unless there is an end to defilements.

How did life start? Is there a beginning to our countless existences? We cannot go back to the past. If we want to know what conditioned our life in the past we should know what it is that conditions our life at the present time. Is there ignorance now, when we see, hear, smell, taste, touch or think? Is there clinging now to nāma and rūpa? So long as we cling to visible objects, sounds, smells, flavours, to things touched and to objects experienced through the mind-door, there are conditions for life to go on. Life is conditioned by ignorance and craving.

We read in the *Discourse pertaining to the Great Sixfold Sense-field* (Middle Length Sayings III, no. 149) that the Buddha, while he was staying near Sāvatthī in the Jeta Grove, said to the monks:

> *Monks, (anyone) not knowing, not seeing eye as it really is, not knowing, not seeing material shapes... visual consciousness... impact on the eye as it really is, and not knowing, not seeing as it really is the feeling, whether pleasant, painful or neither painful nor pleasant, that arises conditioned by impact on the eye, is attached to the eye, is attached to material shapes, is attached to visual consciousness, is attached to impact on the eye; and as for that feeling, whether pleasant, painful or neither painful nor pleasant, that arises*

> *conditioned by impact on the eye–to that too is he attached. While he, observing the satisfaction, is attached, bound and infatuated, the five khandhas of grasping go on to future accumulation. And his craving, which is connected with again-becoming, accompanied by attachment and delight, finding its pleasure here and there, increases in him. And his physical anxieties increase, and mental anxieties increase, and physical torments increase, and mental torments increase, and physical fevers increase, and mental fevers increase. He experiences anguish of body and anguish of mind.*

People wonder whether there is a first cause in the cycle of birth and death. How and when did ignorance first arise? It is of no use to speculate about a first cause, because this does not lead to the goal, which is the eradication of defilements. There is ignorance now; that is a reality. It is conditioned by past ignorance. If it is not eradicated there will be ignorance in the future, forever. Life is like a wheel, turning around, without any beginning.

We do not know from which plane we came, nor where we are going. Life is so short, it is like a dream. We are born with different characters and we have accumulated many defilements. We cannot go back to the past and find out how we accumulated our defilements. People in the past had defilements as well. Some of them could recollect their former lives and see how they accumulated defilements. In the *Therīgāthā* (Psalms of the Sisters, Canto XV, 72, Isidāsi) we read about the life of Isidāsi who had one husband after another but could not please anyone of them. However, she became a bhikkhunī (nun) and she later attained arahatship. She was able to recollect her former lives and she knew then why she had to endure so much sorrow: in a former life she had committed adultery. This akusala kamma caused her to be reborn in hell where she had to stay for many centuries and to be reborn an animal three times. After that she was reborn as a human being three times, but had to suffer great misery in the course of those lives, until she attained arahatship.

Life is birth, old age, sickness and death. The sorrow we all experience in life is unavoidable so long as there are conditions for it. We read in the *Therīgāthā* (Canto VI, 50, Paṭācārā's Five Hundred) about women who suffered the loss of their children. They came to see Paṭācārā who herself had lost in one day her husband, two children, parents and brother. She was mad with grief, but was able to recover. She became a sotāpanna, and later on she attained arahatship. She consoled the bereaved women:[1]

The way by which men come we cannot know;
Nor can we see the path by which they go.
Why mourn then for him who came to you,
Lamenting through your tears: "My son! My son!"
Seeing you do not know the way he came,
Nor yet the manner of his leaving you?
Weep not, for such is here the life of man.
Unasked he came, unbidden did he go from here.
See! Ask yourself again whence came your son
To bide on earth this little breathing space?
By one way come and by another gone,
As man to die, and pass to other births–
So here and so from here–why would you weep?

We do not know from which plane of existence people have come nor where they are going. The number of lives in the past is incalculable and thus it is not surprising that in the course of those lives people have been related to each other in many ways, as parents, brothers, sisters, children. Do we want to continue in the cycle of birth and death? We read in the *Therīgāthā* (Canto VI, 55, Mahā-Pajāpatī) that Mahā-Pajāpatī, who had made an end to defilements, spoke thus:

... Now have I understood how Ill[2] does come.
Craving, the cause, in me is dried up.
Have I not trod, have I not touched the end
Of Ill–the ariyan, the eightfold Path?
Oh! But 'tis long I've wandered down all time.
Living as mother, father, brother, son,
And as grandparent in the ages past–
Not knowing how and what things really are,
And never finding what I needed sore.

---

[1] I am using the translation of the "Thera-therī-gāthā" by Ms. Rhys Davids: Psalms of the Early Buddhists, P.T.S.

[2] Dukkha.

> *But now my eyes have seen the Exalted One;*
> *And now I know this living frame's the last,*
> *And shattered in the unending round of births.*
> *No more Pajāpatī shall come to be!...*

Events in our lives today have their conditions in the past. Tendencies we have now we may have had in the past as well. Deeds we do now we may have performed in the past too. We read in the teachings that the Buddha said of both his own deeds and the deeds of others that similar ones had been performed in the past. We cannot recollect our former lives, but we know that we have accumulated defilements for countless aeons.

Is the word "defilement" not too strong an expression? We may think that we have a pure conscience marred only by a few imperfections and weak points. "Defilement" is the translation of the Pāli term "kilesa". Kilesa is that which is dirty, impure. When we know our own kilesas better we will see their loathsomeness and the sorrow they bring. We will see their dangers, we will realize how deeply rooted they are and how hard to eradicate.

Our life is full of attachment, ill-will and ignorance. Not everybody sees that there will be less sorrow when defilements are eliminated. We each have different expectations in life. We all want happiness but each one of us has a different idea of happiness and the ways to achieve it. Both in the Buddha's time and today there are "foolish people" and "wise people". Foolish people think that it is good to be attached to people and things. They say that one is not really alive if one has no attachment. Because of their ignorance they do not see cause and effect in their lives. When they have pleasant experiences they do not see that these are only moments of vipāka[1] which fall away immediately. When they experience unpleasant things they blame others for their experience; they do not understand that the real cause is within themselves, that the cause is the bad deeds they themselves have performed. Those who suffer mental anxieties and depressions and are destressed about their daily life, try to escape from it in many different ways. Some people find satisfaction in going to the movies. Others take alcoholic drinks or intoxicating drugs in order to live in a

[1] Vipākacitta is the result of kamma. Kusala kamma, good deeds, bring pleasant results and akusala kamma, evil deeds, bring unpleasant results.

different world or to feel like a different person. Those who flee from reality will not know themselves; they will continue to live in ignorance.

In the past and today there are people who reject the Buddha's teachings or who misunderstand them. They do not see that life is conditioned by ignorance and craving. They do not know the way leading to the end of defilements. But those who see that defilements cause sorrow want to have less defilements. They listen to the teachings and apply themselves to dāna (generosity), to sīla (morality) and to bhāvanā (mental development). Few people, however, are inclined to cultivate each day of their lives the wisdom which eradicates defilements. They are wise people.

In the *Thera-therī-gāthā* (Psalms of the Brethren and Sisters) we read about men and women in the Buddha's time who had the same struggles in life, the same anxieties and fears as people today. They had many defilements but they were able to eradicate them by following the eightfold Path. If they could do it, why can we not do it?

Those who are wise understand that life does not last and that it is therefore a matter of urgency to develop the way leading to the end of defilements. People are inclined to delay practising the Buddha's teachings. We read in the *Thera-gāthā* (Mātanga's Son, Canto III, 174):

Too cold! Too hot! Too late! Such is the cry.
And so, past men who shake off work (that waits
Their hand), the fateful moments fly,
But he who reckons cold and heat as less
Than straws, doing his duties as a man,
He no defaulter proves to happiness...

Do we think it is too cold, too hot, too late to be mindful? We always want to do something other than be mindful of the present moment. Is our highest aim in life enjoyment of the things which can be experienced through the senses? Is it wealth, physical comfort, the company of relatives and friends? People forget that none of these things last. They forget that as soon as we are born we are old enough to die. Those who are wise, however, see the impermanence of all conditioned things. In the *Theragāthā* (Canto

II, 145) we read that Vītasoka, when his hair was being dressed by the barber, looked into the mirror and saw some grey hairs. He was reminded of reality and developed insight. While he was sitting there he attained enlightenment. We read:

"Now let him shave me!"— so the barber came.
From him I took the mirror and, therein
Reflected, on myself I gazed and thought:
"Futile for lasting is this body shown."
(Thus thinking on the source that blinds our sight
My spirit's) darkness melted into light,
Stripped are the swathing vestments
(of defilements[1]) utterly.
Now is there no more coming back to be.

A look into the mirror can be most revealing! It can remind us of impermanence. Thus we see that even when we perform the most common activities of daily life we do not have to waste our time; mindfulness can be developed. We may think that our daily tasks prevent us from being mindful, but there are nāma and rūpa presenting themselves through the six doors, no matter what we are doing. Even when one is preparing food, insight can be developed and enlightenment can be attained. We read in the *Therīgāthā* (Canto I, 1) about a woman who was preparing food in the kitchen. A flame burnt the food. She realized at that moment the impermanence of conditioned realities and became then and there, in the kitchen, a non-returner, anāgāmī[2]. She entered the order of bhikkhunīs and attained arahatship later on. She declared her attainment with the following verse:

Sleep softly, little Sturdy, take your rest
At ease, wrapt in the robe you yourself have made.
Stilled are the passions that would rage within,
Withered as potherbs in the oven dried.

---

[1] Here I have added "of defilements", following the Thai translation which uses the word kilesa.

[2] A person who has realized the third stage of enlightenment.

We may think that we cannot be mindful because we are too restless and agitated. It is encouraging for us to read that people in the Buddha's time who were also oppressed by their many defilements and who suffered from their obsessions, could nevertheless attain enlightenment. In the *Therīgāthā* (Canto V, 38, "An Anonymous Sister) we read about a nun who was troubled by sense desires and could not find peace of mind. She was taught Dhamma by Dhammadinnā and she attained the "six supernormal powers", the sixth of which is the destruction of all defilements[1]. The text states:

For five-and twenty years since I came forth.
Not for one moment could my heart attain
The blessedness of calm serenity.
No peace of mind I found. My every thought
Was soaked with the passion of sense desires.
With outstretched arms and shedding futile tears
I went, a wretched woman, to my cell.
Then She to this poor Bhikkhunī drew near,
Who was my foster-mother in the faith.
She taught me the Dhamma, wherein I learnt
The factors, organs, bases of this self,
Impermanent compound. Hearing her words,
Beside her I sat down to meditate.
And now I know the days of the long past,
And clearly shines the Eye Celestial,
I know the thoughts of other minds, and hear
With sublimated sense the sound of things
Ineffable. The mystic potencies
I exercise; and all the deadly Drugs
That poisoned every thought are purged away.
A living truth for me this "Sixfold Knowledge",
Accomplished is the Buddha's Dhamma.

Those who are oppressed by their anxieties to such an extent that

[1] The five "mundane" powers or knowledges are: magical powers, divine ear, by which one hears sounds heavenly and human, far and near, penetration of the minds of others, divine eye, by which one sees the passing away and rebirth of beings, and remembrance of former lives.

they want to flee from reality may even think of committing suicide. In the Buddha's time people were no different from people today. But even for those who have lost all hope there is a way by which they can be freed from despair, liberated from sorrow and fear. We read in the *Therīgāthā* (Canto V, 40, Sīhā) about a nun who was on the point of committing suicide. But at that moment her knowledge reached maturity and she became an arahat. The text states:

Distracted, harassed by desires of sense,
Unmindful of the "What" and "Why" of things,
Stung and inflated by the memories
Of former days, over which I lacked control–
Corrupting canker spreading over my heart–
I followed heedless dreams of happiness,
And got no steadiness of mind,
All given over to dalliance with sense,
So did I fare for seven weary years,
In lean and sallow misery of unrest.
I, wretched, found no ease by day or night,
So took a rope and plunged into the wood:
"Better for me a friendly gallows-tree
Than indulging in a worldly life."
Strong was the noose I made; and on a bough
I bound the rope and flung it round my neck,
When see!... my heart was set at liberty!

When we read about men and women in the Buddha's time we recognize ourselves and other people who are living today. We all have accumulated lobha, dosa and moha. We all are hindered by our many defilements. We sometimes wonder whether we will ever reach the goal. Nibbāna seems to be far away. But in fact, with every moment of right mindfulness of nāma or rūpa right understanding can develop, and thus wrong view can be eliminated and eventually enlightenment be attained. We read in the *Theragāthā* (Canto XVI, 252, Mālunkyā's Son) about the son of Mālunkyā who listened to the Buddha and later attained arahatship. The text states:

Sight of fair shape bewildering mindfulness,
If one but heed the image sweet and dear,
The heart inflamed in feeling does overflow,
And clinging stays. Thus in him do grow
Divers emotions rooted in the sight.
Greed and aversion and the heart of him
Does suffer grievously. Of him, thus heaping
Store of pain and suffering, the Buddha[1] *said:—*
Far from nibbāna!

(The same is said about the impressions through the other senses.)

He who for things he sees, no passion breeds,
But mindful, clear of head, can suffer sense
With uninflamed heart, no clinging stays;
And as he sees, so normally he feels;
For him no heaping up, but diminishing;
So does he heedfully pursue his way.
Of him, building no store of ill, the Buddha said:—
Near is nibbāna!

The Buddha's teachings can change people's character if they walk the way he taught. We read in the *Theragāthā* (Canto II, 139, Nanda) about Nanda, who had attained arahatship. He said:

Heedless and shallow once my thoughts were set
On all the bravery of outward show;
Fickle was I and frivolous; all my days
Were worn with wanton sensuality.
But by the Buddha's skilful art benign,
Who of sun's lineage comes, was I brought
To live by deeper thought, whereby my heart
From (the great swamp of endless) life I drew.

People in the Buddha's time understood how mindfulness should be developed every day of their lives. We read in the "Papañcasūdanī", the commentary to the *Middle Length Sayings*

[1] The English text has here: "we say", but I follow the Thai translation: "The Buddha said".

in the section about the *Satipaṭṭhāna sutta* (Middle Length Sayings I, 10) that the Buddha taught the "Four Applications of Mindfulness"[1] to the people of Kuru (in the District of Delhi). In Kuru all classes of people would develop mindfulness, even the slave-labourers. Those who did not develop mindfulness were considered as dead people. If we do not develop right understanding we are like dead people because we have to continue in the cycle of birth and death.

Those who are ignorant of Dhamma and those who are wise have different aims in life and they also have different views of the future. Some people think of a happy rebirth as the fulfilment of all their expectations in life. They hope for life to continue in heaven where there is bliss forever. Others may not think of an after-life, but they dream of an ideal world in the future, a world without wars, without discord among men. But they do not know how such a world could come into being.

Those who have right understanding of Dhamma know that what we call "world" is impermanent. This world arose by conditions and it will pass away again. World systems arise and dissolve. When it is the appropriate time a person is born who will be a Buddha who teaches the truth. But even the teachings do not stay; they are misinterpreted and corrupted because of people's defilements. People today still have the opportunity to hear Dhamma and develop the eightfold Path. Those who are wise do not dream of an ideal world in the future. They know that the most beneficial thing one can do both for oneself and for others is to eliminate defilements right at the present moment. The Buddha taught mental development to those who want to eliminate defilements. People have different accumulations. Some develop samatha (tranquil meditation), others vipassanā (insight, right understanding of realities); others again develop both samatha and vipassanā. Those who develop vipassanā will know what the world really is; they will know that there are "six worlds": the world of visible object, of sound, of odour, of flavour, of tangible objects and of mental objects. They will know that these worlds are impermanent. The Buddha knew with clear vision all worlds in all ways and

[1] The "Four Applications of mindfulness" are: Mindfulness of the Body, of Feelings, of Cittas and of Dhammas. All nāmas and rūpas which are objects of mindfulness are included in these four "applications".

under every aspect; he is called "Knower of the Worlds" (lokavidū)[1].

Those who still have craving cannot see that the end of rebirth is the end of dukkha. Those who see the impermanence of all conditioned things can eliminate craving stage by stage. The arahat does not cling to life any more. For him there will be an end to life, that is: an end to nāma and rūpa, never to arise again, an end to birth, old age, sickness and death. The arahat realizes that the end to birth is true happiness, true peace. In the *Theragāthā* (Canto XVI, 248) we read that the arahat Adhimutta was assailed by robbers who were amazed by his calmness. Adhimutta said:

... He who has passed beyond, from grasping free,
Whose task is done, sane and immune, is glad,
Not sorry, when the term of lives is reached,
As one who from the slaughter-house escapes.
He who the ideal order has attained,
All the world over seeking nought to own,
As one who from a burning house escapes,
When death is drawing near he grieves not...

Ignorance and clinging condition our life. When ignorance and clinging are eradicated there are no more conditions for rebirth. The end of birth is the end of dukkha. As we have read in the above-quoted *Discourse on the Great Sixfold Sense-field*(Middle Length Sayings III, no 149), the Buddha said about the person who does not see things as they are, that he experiences "anguish of body and anguish of mind". He said about the person who sees things as they are:

But (anyone), monks, knowing and seeing eye as it really is, knowing and seeing material shapes... visual consciousness... impact on the eye as it really is, and knowing, seeing as it really is the feeling, whether pleasant, painful or neither painful nor pleasant, that arises conditioned by impact on the eye, is not attached to the eye nor to material shapes nor to visual consciousness nor to impact on the eye; and that feeling, whether pleasant or painful or neither painful nor pleasant,

[1] See Visuddhimagga VII, 36--46.

that arises conditioned by impact on the eye–neither to that is he attached. While he, observing the peril, is not attached, bound or infatuated, the five khandhas of grasping go on to future diminution. And his craving which is connected with again-becoming, accompanied by attachment and delight, finding its pleasure here and there, decreases in him. And his physical anxieties decrease, and mental anxieties decrease, and bodily torments... and mental torments... and bodily fevers decrease, and mental fevers decrease. He experiences happiness of body and happiness of mind.

Chapter 11

The Development of Calm

If there be none in front, nor none behind
Be found, is one alone and in the woods
Exceeding pleasant does his life become.
Come then! alone I'll get me hence and go
To lead the forest-life the Buddha praised,
And taste the welfare which the brother knows,
Who dwells alone with concentrated mind...

Those were the words of a prince who longed to live in the forest (*Theragāthā*, Canto X, 234, Ekavihāriya). Do we not all have moments when we wish to have none in front and none behind us, moments when we wish to dwell alone? It seems impossible to find tranquillity in daily life. We have people around us the whole day, and there is noise everywhere. The real cause of our restlessness, however, is not outside but inside ourselves; the real cause is our defilements. We may not commit grave crimes such as killing or stealing, but we think unwholesome thoughts and we spend much time in talking about other people's mistakes and shortcomings. We harm ourselves in that way. Unwholesomeness is harmful, to both body and mind. We can see the difference in appearance between a restless person and someone who is serene and full of loving-kindness.

It is not easy to change our habits. If we are used to speaking in an unwholesome way then we cannot expect to change ourselves at once. For how long have we been accumulating unwholesomeness? Because of our accumulated unwholesome tendencies we are hindered in doing good deeds, speaking in a wholesome way and having wholesome thoughts, and we are restless and agitated. We would like to have peace of mind but we do not know where to find it.

Dāna (generosity), sīla (morality) and bhāvanā (mental development) are ways of having kusala cittas instead of akusala cittas.

The Buddha encouraged people to develop all kinds of wholesomeness, be it dāna, sīla or bhāvanā. At the moment of kusala citta there are no lobha, dosa and moha and there is calm. When we offer food to the monks and pay respect to them there is calm. There is not always opportunity for dāna or sīla but there is at any time opportunity for the way of kusala which is mental development, bhāvanā, and this includes: the study and the teaching of Dhamma, samatha (development of calm) and vipassanā. Dāna and sīla can be performed with paññā or without it, but for mental development paññā is indispensable.

As regards the form of bhāvanā which is the study of Dhamma, we will have more understanding of the teachings through reading the Tipiṭaka, the Three Collections of the Vinaya, the Suttanta and the Abhidhamma. If we study the Dhamma, ponder over it and also explain it to others, there are conditions for kusala cittas with paññā. Both our own life and the lives of others will be enriched. The study of the Dhamma will help us to have right understanding of our life.

Samatha, the development of calm, and vipassanā, the development of insight, are included in bhāvanā, but they each have a different aim and a different way of development. The aim of samatha is calm. In samatha defilements are temporarily subdued, but they are not eradicated. The aim of vipassanā is seeing things as they are. The right understanding, paññā, which is developed in vipassanā can eradicate defilements.

Through samatha one develops the calm which is temporary freedom from lobha, attachment, dosa, aversion, and moha, ignorance. When we realize how often in a day there are akusala cittas, we would like to develop more wholesome thoughts. Samatha is a way of developing kusala cittas, also at the moments when there is no opportunity for dāna or sīla. Samatha is a means of developing a higher degree of calm, but one must have right understanding of the way of its development and one must know the characteristic of calm which is wholesome. Some people may think that there is calm when they are alone in the woods, but is that always the calm which is wholesome? Instead of kusala cittas there may be attachment, aversion and ignorance. Thus, in order to develop samatha one must have a very precise knowledge of the different cittas which arise, otherwise one is likely to take for calm what is in fact akusala citta.

For the development of samatha there are specific meditation subjects (kammaṭṭhāna), forty in all[1]. It depends on the individual which subject conditions calm for him. If one would try to use, instead of one or more among these forty meditation subjects, any other object, it would not help one to attain true calm.

Right understanding of the characteristic of calm and of the meditation subject is the most important factor for the development of samatha. One may think that samatha is a matter of just concentrating on one object, but which type of citta arises while one tries to concentrate? Are we attached to an idea of "my concentration"? When the citta is akusala citta there is no mental development. Thus, it is essential to know when the citta is kusala citta and when it is not.

What is concentration? Concentration or one-pointedness, in Pāli "ekaggatā cetasika" or "samādhi", is a mental factor, cetasika[2], which accompanies each citta. Its function is to focus on one object. For example, seeing is a citta which experiences visible object. One-pointedness or ekaggatā cetasika, which accompanies the citta, is focusing on only that object. Each citta can have only one object at a time and ekaggatā cetasika focuses on that object. No matter whether there is seeing, hearing, a citta with attachment, aversion, generosity or wisdom, there is ekaggatā cetasika accompanying these different moments. The quality of ekaggatā cetasika depends on the citta it accompanies. When ekaggatā cetasika accompanies akusala citta it is also akusala, and when it accompanies kusala citta it is also kusala.

As regards right concentration in samatha, this can arise only if there is right understanding of the development of calm. When there is calm there is at the same time right concentration as well which accompanies the kusala citta.

Can samatha be developed in daily life or do we have to lead a secluded life? If one intends to develop higher degrees of calm,

[1] For details see: Visuddhimagga, Ch IV--IX.

[2] Cetasika is a mental factor accompanying citta. There is only one citta at a time, but each citta is accompanied by several cetasikas which each perform their own function. Some cetasikas accompany each citta, others do not. There are akusala cetasikas which accompany only akusala citta, and there are "sobhana cetasikas" (beautiful cetasikas) which accompany only sobhana citta.

there are specific conditions which have to be fulfilled, as we will see. However, not everybody is able to or intends to develop higher degrees of calm. If we have right understanding of samatha, there can also be conditions for moments of calm in daily life. We can, in daily life, reflect for example on the loathsomeness of the body or on corpses, which are among the forty meditation subjects which can condition calm. For some people the meditations on a corpse can be helpful to have less attachment to sense-impressions. We all have to see dead people or dead animals at times. When we have read about the meditations on corpses and pondered over them there is a condition for the arising of wholesome thoughts at such moments, instead of akusala cittas with aversion. We may remember what the Buddha said about the impermanence of all conditioned things.

We read in the *Thera-therīgāthā* (Psalms of the Brethren, Psalms of the Sisters) about people who were restless, who could not find peace of mind. Meditations on corpses and the foulness of the body reminded them of the truth of impermanence. In the *Theragāthā* (Canto VI, 213, Kulla) we read about the monk Kulla who had been infatuated with sense pleasures. The Buddha recommended him to meditate in the charnel field. The meditation on the putrefaction of the body was the condition for him to attain calm to the degree of the first stage of jhāna, absorption. On that basis he developed insight and attained arahatship. The following verses are an expression of his attainment:

Kulla had gone to where the dead lie still
And there he saw a woman's body cast,
Untended in the field, the food of worms.
"Behold the foul compound, Kulla, diseased,
Impure, dripping, exuding, pride of fools."
Grasping the mirror of the holy Norm[1]*,*
To win the vision by its lore revealed,
I saw reflected there, without, within,
The nature of this empty, fleeting frame,
As is this body, so that one was once.
And as that body, so will this one be...

[1] The Dhamma.

Kulla was reminded of the truth and saw things as they are.

There are people for whom the meditation on corpses or on the loathsomeness of the body is not helpful; they may instead be inclined to the recollections of the Buddha, the Dhamma and the Sangha, which are also included among the forty meditation subjects. Or they may recollect "virtue" (sīla) or "generosity" (dāna), which are other meditation subjects. The recollection of generosity may encourage us to more generosity. In the *Visuddhimagga*(VII, 107) we read that the person who starts to develop this recollection should make the following resolution: "From now on, when there is anyone present to receive, I shall not eat even a single mouthful without having given a gift." After he has given a gift he can recollect the following: "It is gain for me, it is great gain for me, that in a generation obsessed by the stain of avarice I abide with my heart free from stain of avarice, and am freely generous and openhanded, that I delight in relinquishing, expect to be asked, and rejoice in giving and sharing." For this recollection one must know the characteristic of generosity; one cannot recollect generosity and one cannot become calm with this meditation subject if one is not generous in one's daily life.

There are meditations which are the "divine abidings" (Brahmavihāras). They are: loving-kindness (mettā), compassion (karuṇā), sympathetic joy (muditā) and equanimity (upekkhā). However, these qualities cannot be one's meditation subjects if one does not practise them in daily life. How could one develop the meditation subject of loving-kindness if one does not know the characteristic of loving-kindness as it appears in daily life? We may have moments of pure loving-kindness but there are bound to be many moments of selfish affection in between. Are we not attached to people? It is necessary to know exactly when there is a moment of pure loving-kindness and when there is attachment. There must be right understanding which clearly distinguishes between these characteristics and thus we see again that right understanding is indispensable for samatha.

If one knows the characteristic of loving-kindness one can develop it and then it can condition calm. This subject can help us to have kusala citta instead of thoughts of ill-will.

Mindfulness of breathing is another meditation subject. In order to develop calm with this subject one must have right understanding of it and know how to be mindful of the characteristic of breath. According to the *Visuddhimagga* mindfulness of breathing is one of the most difficult meditation subjects and, since breath is very subtle, not everyone is able to be mindful of it.

What is breath? What we call breath is rūpa, a physical phenomenon. Rūpas of the body can be conditioned by one of the four following factors: by kamma, by citta, by temperature or by food. Breath is conditioned by citta. So long as there is citta there is breath conditioned by citta. We all cling to our life and all the things we enjoy in life, but life is very fragile. Life is supported by breath, rūpa which arises and then falls away. When we have drawn our last breath, death occurs and of what use are then our possessions and all the things to which we cling so much? When mindfulness of breath is developed with right understanding it can condition the calm which is temporary freedom from defilements. However, the characteristic of breath must be known correctly.

The *Visuddhimagga* (VIII, 197, f.f.) explains that breath appears where it touches the nosetip or upper lip. It falls away immediately at the place where it appears. One should not follow the going out and coming in of breath, one should only be aware of breath where it touches the nosetip or upper lip. The *Visuddhimagga* explains this by way of similes, one of which is the simile of a gate-keeper:

> *This is the simile of the gate-keeper: just as a gate-keeper does not examine people inside and outside the town, asking, "Who are you? Where have you come from? Where are you going? What have you got in your hand?"— for those people are not his concern–but does examine each man as he arrives at the gate, so too, the incoming breaths that have gone inside and the outgoing breaths that have gone outside are not this bhikkhu's concern, but they are his concern each time they arrive at the (nostril) gate itself.*

If one follows the going out and the coming in of breath one's mind will, according to the *Visuddhimagga*(VIII, 197) be "distracted by disquiet and perturbation". Right understanding of the method of development of this subject is indispensable. If one thinks that all that is necessary is just trying very hard to concentrate on breath one may concentrate with lobha, dosa and moha. If one enjoys watching one's breath and if one aims at feeling relaxed there is attachment and this is not bhāvanā. Some people may be inclined to do breathing exercises for their health, but, if one wants to develop calm one must know what is bhāvanā and what is not bhāvanā. The aim of this meditation subject is calm which is wholesome and thus there must be paññā which knows exactly when the citta is kusala citta and when it is akusala citta. When there are moments of calm there is no clinging.

It is extremely difficult to be mindful of breath in the right way so that there can be true calm, freedom from lobha, dosa and moha. It may happen that one takes for breath what is not breath, the rūpa conditioned by citta. Some people follow the movement of the abdomen and they erroneously take this for mindfulness of breath. If one has no accumulations for mindfulness of breath, one should not force oneself to take up this subject. There are many other subjects of meditation which can condition calm.

There can be mindfulness of breath both in samatha and in vipassanā. What is the difference between the object of mindfulness in samatha and the object of mindfulness in vipassanā? In samatha there is sati which is mindful, non-forgetful, of breath in order to temporarily subdue defilements. In samatha the object of mindfulness is not, as is the case in vipassanā, the characteristic of whatever nāma or rūpa appears at the present moment through one of the six doors. There is paññā in both samatha and vipassanā, but the paññā in samatha does not know nāma and rūpa as they are, as non-self (anattā). The paññā in samatha knows when the citta is kusala citta and when it is akusala citta; it knows how to develop the calm which is temporary freedom from defilements. The aim of vipassanā is seeing things as they are. In vipassanā right understanding is developed of all nāmas and rūpa which appear, no matter what one's activities are. Also when one develops calm by means of mindfulness of breathing there are nāmas and rūpas which appear and these can be known as they really are: as impermanent and non-self. The paññā of vipassanā knows nāma and rūpa as they are.

Several of the meditation subjects of samatha can be our recollections in daily life and they can condition moments of calm. Some people, however, may have accumulations to develop higher degrees of calm, even to the stage of jhāna, absorption. When there is a higher degree of calm ekaggatā cetasika or samādhi (concentration) which accompanies the citta with calm is of a higher degree as well. Samādhi develops when there are the right conditions, one cannot force oneself to become concentrated.

In the development of samatha there are three stages of samādi: the preliminary stage or parikamma samādhi, access concentration or upacāra samādhi and attainment concentration or appanā samādi, which accompanies jhānacitta. When there is still the preliminary stage of samādhi, parikamma samādhi, the citta is aware of the meditation subject, but it is not jhānacitta; it is citta of the sensuous plane of consciousness, kāmāvacara citta. Kāmāvacara cittas are the cittas which arise in daily life when, for example, we see, think or wish for something. When samādhi has reached the stage of access concentration, upacāra samādhi, there is a higher degree of calm but at that stage the citta is still kāmāvacara citta, not jhānacitta. When samādhi has reached the stage of attainment concentration, appanā samādhi, the citta is jhānacitta. The jhānacitta experiences the meditation subject with absorption; at that moment one is free from sense-impressions and thus also from the defilements which are bound up with them. The jhānacitta is of a higher level of consciousness than kāmāvacara citta.

If people do not know about the different stages of samādhi they may erroneously think that they have jhānacittas or they may doubt whether they have attained jhāna or not. The jhānacitta is accompanied by paññā. If one has doubts it is clear that there is no paññā. Even if one has no intention to cultivate jhāna it is useful to know about the different degrees of samādhi. One might have cultivated jhāna in a past life and if there are the right conditions, one of the degrees of samādhi could arise. People who have not studied Dhamma may have confused ideas about concentration and about jhāna. There is right concentration and wrong concentration. When people concentrate on a meditation subject in the wrong way, for example with lobha, there is wrong concentration. They may, because of wrong concentration, have unusual experiences which they take for jhāna. Or they may even take such experiences for the attainment of nibbāna.

There are several stages of jhāna and each higher stage is more subtle and more refined than the preceding one. There is rūpa-jhāna, which is translated as "fine-material jhāna", and arūpa-jhāna, which is translated as "immaterial jhāna". Arūpa-jhāna is more subtle than rūpa-jhāna; the meditation subjects of arūpa-jhānacitta do not pertain to objects which can be experienced through the senses.

Of the forty meditation subjects, some can lead only to access concentration, upacāra samādhi, some to rūpa-jhāna but not to the highest stage, and some lead to the highest stage of rūpa-jhāna. There are four (or, for some people five) stages of rūpa-jhāna[1] Those who see the disadvantages of the meditation subjects of rūpa-jhāna, which are less refined than those of arūpa-jhāna, develop the meditation subjects of arūpa-jhāna. There are four stages of arūpa-jhāna, which are: the sphere of boundless space, the sphere of boundless consciousness, the sphere of nothingness and the sphere of neither-perception-nor-non-perception. Perception in the fourth arūpa-jhāna is very subtle.

Of those who develop samatha only very few can attain jhāna. Much skill has to be developed in order to attain jhāna. One should know the conditions for the attainment of jhāna and what can obstruct its attainment. We read in the *Visuddhimagga* (XII, 8) how difficult it is to attain the preliminary stage of samādhi, parikamma samādhi, or access concentration, upacāra samādhi, to attain jhāna and to develop the skills in jhāna in order to acquire supernatural powers.

People today want to experience something which is beyond this world because they feel distressed about life or they are bored. Wouldn't we sometimes like to know the future? We may be curious as to what fortune-tellers can predict about our life. Many of us read the horoscope in the daily newspaper, and even when we say that we do not believe in those things we cannot help attaching some importance to them. Sick people who cannot be cured by a doctor go to healers who claim that they can treat diseases in a more effective way than doctors. We may well go to fortune-tellers, or to people who claim to have clairvoyance, but

[1] For the attainment of jhāna one has to develop jhāna-factors, specific cetasikas. At each higher stage of rūpa-jhāna jhāna-factors are abandoned, they are no longer needed. Some people can at the second stage abandon two factors instead of one factor and thus for them there are four stages of jhāna instead of five stages.

we still do not know ourselves. We still have defilements, we still have ignorance, we still have to continue in the cycle of birth and death. So long as there are attachment, ill-will and ignorance in one's heart, true happiness cannot be found.

In the Buddha's time people developed jhāna until they became quite skilful and they even acquired supernatural powers. Those who have attained the highest stage of rūpa-jhāna and of arūpa-jhāna and have acquired "mastery" in the attainment of the these stages, can apply themselves to the development of supernatural powers. The development of those powers is extremely difficult; only very few of those who attain jhāna can develop them. The supernatural powers developed by means of samatha are: miraculous powers such as flying through the air, walking on water, diving into the earth; the "Celestial Ear" or clairaudiance; the power to discern the thoughts of others; the power of recollecting one's past lives; the "Celestial Eye" (claivoyance), by means of which one also sees the passing away and rebirth of beings.

We read in the *Discourse on the Fruits of the Life of a Recluse* (Dialogues of the Buddha I, no. 2, 77, 78) that the Buddha spoke to the King of Magadha about the recluse who had supernatural powers. The Buddha said to the King:

> *With his heart thus serene, made pure, translucent, cultured, devoid of evil, supple, ready to act, firm and imperturbable, he applies and bends down his mind to the modes of the Wondrous Gift. He enjoys the Wondrous Gift in its various modes–being one he becomes many, or having become many he becomes one again; he becomes visible or invisible; he goes, feeling no obstruction, to the further side of a wall or rampart or hill, as if through air; he penetrates up and down through solid ground, as if through water; he walks on water without breaking through, as if on solid ground; he travels crosslegged in the sky, like birds on wing; even the Moon and the Sun, so powerful, so mighty though they be, does he touch and feel with his hand; he reaches in the body even up to the heaven of Brahmā...*

In Buddhism one learns to study cause and effect. People are impressed by extraordinary things when they do not know the conditions that give rise to them. Each phenomenon in our life has conditions through which it arises. When we know this we are not surprised by strange phenomena. Moggallāna, Anuruddha and other disciples has supernatural powers, but they did not cling to them or take them for self because they realized that those phenomena arose because of conditions.

Samatha is a high degree of kusala kamma and it brings about kusala vipāka. Samatha can help people to be more calm. But defilements cannot be eradicated by samatha, even if calm is developed to the degree of jhāna. Nor can defilements be eradicated by supernatural powers. Jhāna and supernatural powers do not lead to the end of ignorance. The Buddha, when he was still a Bodhisatta, developed samatha, but he also developed vipassanā in order to become the Fully Enlightened One, the Buddha.

In the *Vinaya* (Book of the Discipline I, Pārājika, Defeat I, 1, 4) we read that the Buddha spoke to the brahmin of Verañja about the "three watches" of the night in which he attained enlightenment. In the first watch he recollected, by means of supernatural powers developed through samatha, his former lives. In the second watch he saw, by means of supernatural powers, the passing away and rebirth of beings. In the third watch his defilements were eradicated and he attained Buddhahood. We read:

> *Then with mind collected... I directed the mind towards the knowledge of the destruction of the cankers. I knew as it really is: This is dukkha, this is the arising of dukkha, this is the stopping of dukkha, this is the course leading to the stopping of dukkha... In me, thus knowing, thus seeing, my mind was freed from the canker of sensual pleasures, my mind was freed from the canker of becoming, my mind was freed from the canker of false views, my mind was freed from the canker of ignorance. (To me) freed, came knowledge through the freedom; I knew: Destroyed is rebirth, lived is the Brahma-life, done is what was to be done, there is no beyond for this state of things. This was, brahmin, the third knowledge attained by me in the third watch of the night. Ignorance was dispelled, knowledge arose, darkness was dispelled, light arose...*

The four ariyan truths can be known through vipassanā. How could one know that nāma and rūpa are dukkha unless one is mindful of their characteristics when they appear at the present moment? Only thus will we know that they are impermanent and dukkha, unsatisfactory. This kind of knowledge leads to the eradication of defilements.

Chapter 12

Vipassanā

Questioner: In the development of vipassanā, insight, we learn to see things as they are. Seeing things as they are means: seeing nāma and rūpa as they are. Thus, we should distinguish nāma and rūpa from each other more clearly. Rūpa is that which does not experience anything. Can we say that nāma is that which experiences and rūpa is that which is experienced?

Nina: You say that rūpa is that which is experienced. Your words imply that nāma cannot be experienced. Nāma experiences not only rūpa but it experiences nāma as well. Can you not notice it when there is a happy feeling, when there is aversion, when there is thinking? It is not "self" who notices this, but nāma. Nāma knows nāma at those moments.

Question: In vipassanā we develop awareness. Awareness is always awareness of something. I am not sure that I understand what awareness is.

Nina: The Pāli term "sati" is translated into English as "mindfulness" or "awareness". These words might create confusion. When we say in conventional language that we are aware of something it might mean that we know or experience something, but this does not necessarily mean that there is sati. It is, however, not important which word we use to name the reality which is sati, but it is essential to understand its characteristic.

Sati is a "beautiful" mental factor, sobhana cetasika, which arises only with sobhana cittas[1]. Each kusala citta is accompanied by sati which is non-forgetful, heedful, of what is wholesome and prevents one from unwholesomeness. There are many degrees and levels of sati. There is sati with dāna, generosity. When we are generous it is sati which is non-forgetful of generosity. There is sati with sīla, morality. When we abstain from killing it is sati

[1] Sobhana cittas include not only kusala cittas but also kusala vipākacittas and kiriyacittas (inoperative cittas) of the arahat, accompanied by sobhana hetus, beautiful roots.

which is heedful, which prevents us from killing. There is sati in samatha, the development of calm. When we for example ponder over the virtues of the Buddha there are moments of calm; it is sati which is mindful of the object which conditions calm. When we develop vipassanā there is sati accompanying the kusala citta, and it is mindful of whatever nāma or rūpa appears now, at this moment, through one of the six doors. Through mindfulness of nāma and rūpa we will learn to see things as they really are. Thus, no matter whether we perform dāna, observe sīla, develop samatha or vipassanā, there is sati with the kusala citta, but the quality of sati is different at these different moments.

Question: How do I know when there is sati of vipassanā?

Nina: In order to know when there is sati of vipassanā we should understand what the *objectof sati* is: a reality, a nāma or rūpa which appears now. Nāmas and rūpas appear one at a time through the six doors. They are realities which can be directly experienced. We are ignorant of realities and we do not know the difference between realities and concepts or ideas. We can think of concepts and ideas but they are not realities which can be directly experienced through one of the six doors. We believe that there are people and things which stay and we do not see that what we take for permanent or self are in reality only different phenomena which are impermanent and not self.

We cling to the concept of a person or thing which exists, but what is there in reality? What can be directly experienced through one of the six doors? Not a person, not a thing which exists, only different elements which present themselves one at a time through eyes, ears, nose, tongue, bodysense or mind, through these six doorways.

When we, for example, take a loaf of bread, there is usually no development of insight, but we cling to the concept of a bread which stays, at least for some time. Bread is a concept or idea, it is not a reality which can be directly experienced. What are the realities which can be directly experienced? Through the eyes that which is visible, visible object, can be experienced. We do not see a loaf of bread, but we can think of bread because of remembrance of past experiences. The seeing of visible object conditions the thinking of the concept of bread. Through the eyes appears only visible object. Seeing sees visible object. Visible object and seeing are realities which can be known by paññā, right understanding. When we touch the loaf of bread, tangible object can be experienced through the bodysense, namely: hardness, softness, heat, cold, motion or pressure. These are realities, rūpas, which can be known by paññā. The nāma which experiences these rūpas is also real and it can be known by paññā. Through the nose odour can be experienced. The rūpa which is odour and the nāma which experiences odour are realities which can be known by paññā. Through the tongue flavour can be experienced. The rūpa which is flavour and the nāma which experiences flavour are realities which can be known. Thus we see that there are many different nāmas and rūpas which can be known one at a time. We still think: "I see, I hear, I experience", but through the development of insight we will learn that there are only nāma and rūpa, no self. The nāma which is seeing sees, not self. Seeing arises because of conditions and falls away immediately, although we do not realize this. The nāma which is hearing hears, not self. There are many different types of nāmas which experience different objects.

One nāma or rūpa at a time can be object of mindfulness, not concepts or ideas such as a person, a cup or a loaf of bread. We use names in daily life which denote concepts and ideas, but we must know the difference between concepts and ideas and characteristics of nāma and rūpa which can be directly experienced without the need to name them. Namā and rūpa are ultimate or absolute realities (paramattha dhammas) which each have their own characteristic. Seeing, for example has its own characteristic; we can use different names in different languages to denote seeing, but its characteristic is unchangeable. Seeing is always seeing, no matter how we name it; it is a nāma which experiences visible object and it can be known when it appears. Is there no seeing now? Hardness is always hardness, no matter how we name it; it is a rūpa which can be experienced through the bodysense. Is there no hardness now? Thus, we can use different names for a nāma or a rūpa, but their characteristics cannot be changed. When they appear through one of the six doors they can be directly experienced. We can think of concepts and ideas, but they are not ultimate realities. When we think of them the thinking itself is a reality which arises, a type of nāma; it arises because of conditions.

Sati in vipassanā is mindful, non-forgetful, of ultimate realities, of the nāmas and rūpas which appear. It is completely different from what we mean by "mindfulness" or "awareness" in conventional language. Every citta experiences an object, it is "aware" or conscious of an object, but not every citta is accompanied by sati. Hardness, for example, can be experienced by different types of citta, but there is not sati with every type of citta. When there is sati which is mindful of the characteristic of hardness, only that characteristic appears and there is at that moment no thought of a thing which is hard or of a hand which touches something hard. A thing which is hard or a hand which touches something hard are concepts we may think of, but at such moments there is no mindfulness of the characteristic of hardness. At the moment sati is mindful of hardness which appears, paññā can investigate that characteristic in order to know it as it is: only a rūpa, not a thing which stays, not a "self".

In the beginning there cannot yet be a clear understanding of nāma and rūpa, but through mindfulness of the characteristics of nāma and rūpa which appear one at a time, paññā can gradually develop.

It is important to know the difference between the moments when there is sati and those when there is no sati. There is often forgetfulness of realities, but sometimes sati can arise. We will learn the difference from experience. After there has been forgetfulness of realities for a long time sati may arise which is mindful of one characteristic of nāma or rūpa at a time. It is not self who is mindful, it is sati. We cannot force sati to arise because it is a type of nāma and not self. It can arise only when there are conditions for its arising.

Question: We cannot be aware of nāma and rūpa at the same time, but I would like to know how nāma and rūpa are related to each other. When there is hearing there is also sound which is rūpa. When there is seeing there is also visible object which is rūpa.

Nina: Do you want to have theoretical knowledge of all nāmas and rūpas or do you want to develop the wisdom which knows from direct experience the characteristics of the phenomena appearing through the five senses and through the mind-door? There are different levels of wisdom and we should find out what kind of wisdom we are developing.

There are several kinds of rūpa, some of which are conditioned by kamma, some by citta, some by temperature and some by nutrition. There are many kinds of nāma. Nāma can condition rūpa and rūpa can condition nāma in many different ways.

Question: Why do you use the word "condition"? Is condition the same as cause?

Nina: When we speak about cause we usually think of one cause which brings about one effect. There are, however, different kinds of conditions for each nāma and for each rūpa. For example, when there is seeing, the rūpa which is visible object conditions the seeing by way of object. But seeing does not only have visible object as its condition. Eye-sense, which is another kind of rūpa, conditions the seeing too. In studying the teachings we will know more about the different conditions and we will see how complex the way is in which they operate each time we experience an object. When we know that there are various factors which condition the arising of phenomena such as seeing or hearing, we will better understand, at least in theory, that seeing or hearing are only conditioned phenomena and that they do not belong to a self.

We should know, however, what kind of wisdom we want to develop; do we want to develop only theoretical understanding of the truth, acquired by thinking about it, or do we also want to develop the wisdom which knows the truth through direct experience?

Question: I do not understand the difference between thinking about the truth and the direct experience of the truth. How can we directly experience the truth?

Nina: The truth can be known from direct experience; however, it is not "self" who knows it, but paññā. Paññā can directly know different characteristics of nāma and rūpa when they appear. When we, for example, are feeling hot, and sati is mindful of the characteristic of heat, it can be realized by paññā as a kind of rūpa. It is not necessary to think about it. At the moment we think about it or we call it "rūpa", the characteristic of heat cannot be known. Only what appears at the present moment can be directly known. Knowledge acquired from the direct experience of realities is deeper than knowledge acquired from thinking.

Question: When there is seeing, the seeing is conditioned by the rūpa which is visible object and by the rūpa which is eyesense. Could I experience the rūpas which condition the seeing?

Nina: It is important to remember that we can experience only the nāma or the rūpa which appears at the present moment; not the nāma or rūpa which does not appear. It depends on one's accumulations and on the development of wisdom which types of nāma and rūpa can be directly understood. It is impossible to regulate which nāmas and rūpas we should be aware of and in which order.

Question: Is it right that we should not name realities when we are aware of them, since they have fallen away by the time we name them?

Nina: Is thinking of the name a reality? Does it appear?

Question: Yes, it appears, it is a kind of nāma. We cannot help it that this kind of nāma appears.

Nina: That is right, it arises because of its own conditions. Do you not think that this reality can be known as well? When there is seeing, the characteristic of seeing can be known. When there is thinking about seeing, there is a kind of nāma which is different from seeing. If we try to regulate awareness and think that there should or should not be awareness of particular realities, we do not realize that awareness is anattā, non-self. Nāma and rūpa arise because of their own conditions, they are beyond control. If we try to control sati we will not know realities as they are.

Question: I still think that it is better not to think of the names of phenomena. Am I right?

Nina: There is no need to think of their names; the characteristics of nāma and rūpa can be directly experienced. But if the nāma arises which thinks of a name, we cannot prevent it; thinking is a reality which has its own characteristic and it can be known too.

Question: I have heard that the four Applications of Mindfulness or "satipaṭṭhāna" are: mindfulness of the body, mindfulness of feelings, mindfulness of cittas and mindfulness of dhammas. How can I be aware in accordance with the four Applications of Mindfulness?

Nina: There is no need to think of the four Applications of Mindfulness when we are aware of nāma and rūpa. We can develop understanding only of the reality which appears at the present moment. The Buddha taught the four Applications of Mindfulness in order to show people that all nāmas and rūpas can be object of mindfulness. This does not mean that we should think of those four Applications when we are aware. We cannot control which nāma or rūpa will appear; they are anattā, non-self.

Question: Can what we call the "ego" be the object of mindfulness? In which Application of Mindfulness is it included?

Nina: Where is your "ego" and what is its characteristic? How do you experience it and through which door? Do you experience it through eyes, ears, nose, tongue, bodysense or mind-door?

Question: I can only think of the self but I cannot directly experience its characteristic.

Nina: We can think of many different things, but the reality of that moment is only thinking. In the development of insight we learn that what we take for self are only nāma and rūpa which arise and fall away. In reality there is nothing else besides nāma and rūpa. Since there is no "ego" it is not included in any of the four Applications of Mindfulness.

Question: What about realities outside ourselves, can we have wrong view about them?

Nina: Can you give an example of realities outside ourselves?

Question: I mean things such as a bottle, a table or a chair.

Nina: Things such as a bottle, a table or a chair are not ultimate realities, they are concepts we can think of. Because of ignorance and wrong view we take them for lasting things which are real. It is important to know the difference between ultimate realities, nāma and rūpa, which have each their own characteristic, and concepts. What we take for a bottle, a table or a chair are in reality different kinds of rūpas which arise and fall away. Rūpas which fall away are replaced by new ones so long as there are conditions for them.

The wrong understanding of reality can only be eliminated if the characteristics of nāma and rūpa are known when they appear one at a time through the different doorways.

Question: I heard of people who concentrate on the movement of the abdomen. They say that sometimes there is awareness of the arising and falling of rūpa and sometimes there is awareness of the knowing of the arising and falling of rūpa. Is this the right way of developing awareness?

Nina: What we call abdomen is in reality many different kinds of rūpa. Sati can be aware of only one characteristic of rūpa at a time. For example, through the bodysense we can experience the characteristics of hardness, softness, heat, cold, motion and pressure, but we can experience only one of these characteristics at a time.

Question: When we experience the rūpa which is motion do we not experience the arising and falling away of rūpa?

Nina: In the development of vipassanā there are several stages of insight-knowledge (vipassanā ñāṇa). The first stage is knowing through direct experience the difference between the characteristic of nāma and the characteristic of rūpa (in Pāli: nāma-rūpa-pariccheda-ñāṇa). At the attainment of this stage there is no doubt about the difference between the characteristic of nāma and the characteristic of rūpa which appear at that moment. The development of vipassanā, however, has to continue in order to have a clearer understanding of nāma and rūpa. Only at a later stage can the arising and falling away of nāma and rūpa be known. This stage cannot be attained unless the previous stages have been realized. How could there be direct understanding of the arising and falling away of a nāma or a rūpa if the difference between the characteristics of nāma and rūpa is not clearly discerned first?

Question: Is the arising and falling away of rūpa faster than the movement of the abdomen?

Nina: Nāmas and rūpas arise and fall away extremely rapidly. For example, it seems that there can be seeing and hearing at the same time. In reality this is not so. Hearing can arise very closely after seeing, but when there is hearing, the seeing has fallen away already since there can be only one citta at a time. From this example we see that cittas arise and fall away very rapidly, succeeding one another. Although we know that realities arise and fall away, we do not have yet direct understanding of this truth. The understanding of the different characteristics of nāma and rūpa has to become keener and keener. Only when insight is highly developed can there be direct understanding of the arising and falling away of nāma and rūpa.

Question: How can understanding become keener?

Nina: Only by being aware of nāmas and rūpas when they appear, one at a time. Is there not seeing now, or hearing now? If one tries to concentrate on particular nāmas and rūpas there is only thinking, not the direct knowledge of whatever reality appears at the present moment. Realities such as seeing, hearing, hardness or thinking arise because of their own conditions, we cannot regulate their arising. Should we not know their characteristics? Or should we continue to remain ignorant of them? If we try to concentrate on one nāma or rūpa we are clinging and this will not lead to detachment from the concept of self.

Question: It seems that we have to be aware of so many different nāmas and rūpas.

Nina: We have to be aware of nāma and rūpa over and over again in order to become detached from the notion of self. It is not sufficient to be aware of only one kind of nāma or rūpa. There should be awareness of whatever reality appears. If there is right awareness, without the concept of self who has awareness, this will be a condition for paññā to gradually know more nāmas and rūpas. There is no self who can control anything.

Question: I can see that it is useful to know in theory about the difference between nāma and rūpa. But when we are aware of nāma and rūpa I am inclined to think that it is not necessary to distinguish between them; I doubt whether that will help us to become detached from the concept of self.

Nina: How can there be a precise knowledge of realities if we cannot realize the difference between nāma, the reality which experiences something, feels or remembers, and rūpa, the reality which does not experience anything? If we do not realize the difference between nāma and rūpa we confuse, for example, hearing, which is nāma, and sound, which is rūpa. When there is hearing there is also sound, but sati can be mindful of only one characteristic at a time. Sometimes there may be mindfulness of hearing, sometimes of sound. If we do not know which characteristic appears, hearing or sound, it is clear that we are still ignorant of the reality appearing at the present moment.

Question: The reality of the present moment falls away so quickly, how can we ever catch it?

Nina: If we try to "catch" a reality, we do not have the right understanding and thus the truth will not be known. Realities are experienced through six doorways, but if insight has not been developed we cannot clearly know which reality is experienced through which doorway. So long as there is no precise knowledge of the characteristics of realities, there can be no detachment from the concept of self. When insight is more developed, paññā will know which reality is experienced through which doorway.

Question: Is it difficult to know that a reality is nāma or that it is rūpa? It does not seem very difficult.

Nina: You may think that it is very simple to know that seeing is a kind of nāma, different from visible object which is rūpa, but are you sure as to what appears at the present moment, whether it is nāma or rūpa? Is there sati and of what is it mindful?

Question: I am not sure about the reality appearing at the present moment. It seems as if seeing and visible object appear at the same time.

Nina: Awareness can be aware of only one reality at a time. When it seems to us that seeing and visible object "appear" at the same time, then there is no sati, there is only thinking about phenomena. When one has not yet developed precise understanding of realities, they are not known as they appear one at a time. One may know in theory that nāma is different from rūpa, but that is not the paññā which leads to detachment from the concept of self.

The difference between the nāma and rūpa which appear should be known, but we should not try to "catch" the reality of the present moment. When we have just started to develop insight, there cannot yet be a clear understanding of realities. When there has been mindfulness time and again of characteristics of realities, paññā will develop until it is so keen that we do not take realities for self anymore.

Chapter 13

The Eightfold Path

Questioner: I understand that awareness or mindfulness is useful; but I still do not know how to be mindful in daily life. I feel I have no time for it; I have to do my work.

Nina: The development of insight, vipassanā, is precisely the development of right understanding of ourselves, of our daily life. However, it seems that people want to know many other things but not themselves. Are we afraid of knowing ourselves? The Buddha pointed out that knowing ourselves is more beneficial than knowing other things.

We read in the *Visuddhimagga* (XII, 82) that the Buddha so acted that King Mahā-Kappina and his retinue were invisible to the queen who had followed him with one thousand women attendants and who was sitting nearby. We read:

> *...And when it was asked, "Have you seen the king, venerable sir?", he asked: "But which is better for you, to seek the king or to seek yourself?" She replied, "Myself, venerable sir". Then he likewise taught her the Dhamma as she sat there, so that, together with the thousand women attendants, she became established in the fruition of stream entry (sotāpanna), while the ministers reached the fruition of non-return (anāgāmī), and the king that of arahatship.*

The development of insight should not be separated from daily life; it is precisely in our daily life that insight, right understanding of realities, should be developed. There should be awareness of nāmas and rūpas which appear in our daily life. Thus we develop the eightfold Path. If people say that they have no time to develop insight they have not understood what the eightfold Path is.

Question: What exactly is the eightfold Path? Is it the same as mindfulness? Is it essential for the attainment of enlightenment? Will it make us happier and does it help us to fulfil our duties better?

Nina: When we speak about a reality we should know what type of reality it is, otherwise we cannot have a clear understanding of it. Which ultimate reality, paramattha dhamma[1], is the eightfold Path? There are four paramattha dhammas:

citta (consciousness)
cetasika (mental factor arising with the citta)
rūpa (physical phenomena)
nibbāna

The eightfold Path consists of eight factors and these are cetasikas. They are sobhana cetasikas (beautiful mental factors) arising with the sobhana citta which is mindful of a characteristic of nāma or rūpa. In being mindful of nāma and rūpa the eightfold Path is developed. At the attainment of enlightenment the eight factors arise with the lokuttara citta, "supramundane citta", which experiences nibbāna. Then the Path is lokuttara. When the factors of the eightfold Path do not arise with the lokuttara citta the Path is "lokiya", "mundane".

You asked me whether the eightfold Path is the same as mindfulness. Mindfulness, sati, is one of the factors of the eightfold Path; it is called "sammā-sati"[2] or "right mindfulness". As we have seen, sati arises with sobhana citta. Sati is sammā-sati of the eightfold Path when it arises with the paññā, wisdom, which understands a characteristic of nāma or rūpa appearing through one of the six doors. Any time there is mindfulness of a characteristic of nāma or rūpa which appears, the eightfold Path is being developed.

Question: Thus, the object of the eightfold Path has to be any characteristic of nāma or rūpa which appears through one of the six doors, is that right?

Nina: That is right. A person or a tree are concepts or ideas we can think of, but they are not ultimate realities which appear one at a time through the six doors. Only ultimate realities are the

[1] A reality with its own unchangeable characteristic which can be known through direct experience when it presents itself through one of the six doors. It is different from concepts or ideas of which we may think, but which are not real in the ultimate sense.

[2] Sammā means: right.

object of the eightfold Path. Seeing is a reality with its own unchangeable characteristic which can be directly known, without the need to think about it. Seeing is a nāma which experiences visible object, that which appears through eyesense; there is no person who sees. Hearing is another reality with its own unchangeable characteristic; it can be directly known when it appears. Hearing is a nāma which experiences sound through earsense; there is no person who hears. If we learn to see nāma and rūpa as they are the wrong view of self will be eradicated.

Question: I have learned that the objects of the eightfold Path are those of the Four Applications of Mindfulness or "satipaṭṭhāna" which are the application of mindfulness of the body, of feelings, of cittas and of dhammas. Is sound included in the objects of mindfulness?

Nina: Is sound real?

Question: It is real.

Nina: Why is it real?

Question: Anybody can experience sound through the ears.

Nina: Since sound is a reality which can be experienced can there not be awareness of it?

Question: Yes, there can be awareness of it.

Nina: Sound is an object of mindfulness or satipaṭṭhāna because it is a reality with its own characteristic which can be experienced. If there is mindfulness of the characteristic of sound more often, we will learn that it is only a kind of rūpa which can be experienced through the ear-door and which is different from the nāma which experiences sound.

Question: What about unhappy feeling, is it also object of mindfulness?

Nina: Is it real?

Question: Certainly.

Nina: Thus it is object of mindfulness or satipaṭṭhāna. All realities which can be experienced through the six doors can be objects of mindfulness or satipatthāna.

As regards your question whether the eightfold Path is essential for the attainment of enlightenment: it is essential, there is no other way. When one attains the first stage of enlightenment, the stage of the sotāpanna, the wrong view of self is eradicated completely. The clinging to the concept of self can be eradicated only if we develop the wisdom which clearly knows that all phenomena in us and around us are only nāma and rūpa and nothing else but nāma and rūpa. Thus realities will be known as they are.

You also asked me whether the eightfold Path will make us happier, whether it helps us to fulfil our duties better. Our own defilements make us unhappy and at times we find life very difficult. In developing the eightfold Path we do not immediately eradicate defilements but we acquire a clearer understanding of our life. When there is less clinging to the notion of self, there is less darkness in our life. Right understanding is to the benefit of both ourselves and others. When we have more understanding of our own life we will also have more understanding of others. Through the development of satipaṭṭhāna there can gradually be more conditions for kusala cittas with kindness and compassion. When we do our daily tasks with kusala cittas do you not think that they are performed better?

Question: You explained that the eight factors of the Path are eight sobhana cetasikas, beautiful mental factors. Do all eight factors have to arise with the citta which is mindful?

Nina: Not all eight factors arise together when the citta is not lokuttara citta, "supramundane citta" experiencing nibbāna. When lokuttara citta arises at the attainment of enlightenment all eight factors accompany the citta.

Question: What is the first factor of the eightfold Path?

Nina: The first factor is sammā-diṭṭhi, right view or right understanding. Sammā-diṭṭhi is the kind of paññā which directly understands a characteristic of nāma or rūpa, appearing through one of the six doors. Without right understanding of nāma and rūpa and of the way to develop the eightfold Path enlightenment cannot be attained.

We read in the *Kindred Sayings* (V, Book XII, Kindred Sayings about the Truths, Ch IV, § 7, The Parable of the Sun) that right view is the "forerunner" of full comprehension of the four noble Truths. The four noble Truths are realised at the attainment of enlightenment. We read that the Buddha said:

> *Monks, just as the dawn is the forerunner, the harbinger, of the arising of the sun, even so is right view the forerunner, the harbinger, of fully comprehending the four Ariyan truths.*

> *Of a monk who has right view it may be expected that he will understand as it really is: This is dukkha... this is the arising of dukkha... this is the ceasing of dukkha... this is the way leading to the ceasing of dukkha.*
>
> *Wherefore, monks, an effort must be made to realise: This is dukkha, this is the arising of dukkha, this is the ceasing of dukkha, this is the way leading to the ceasing of dukkha.*

We should know to what end we wish to develop the eightfold Path. Why do you want to develop it?

Question: I want to develop it in order to eradicate defilements such as anger, jealousy, stinginess, and all other kinds of impurities–in other words, everything which is degrading and immoral.

Nina: People think that vipassanā can solve all their problems at once and they believe that defilements can be eradicated immediately. But for how many lives have we accumulated defilements? Since these lives are countless how could we eradicate defilements immediately? So long as we are not yet ariyans the aim of our development of vipassanā is to know the truth about ourselves, in order to eradicate the wrong view of self. We have to be so very patient. We should not forget the sutta about the knife-handle (Kindred Sayings III, Middle Fifty, Ch V, § 101, Adze-handle), where we read that the Buddha said:

> *... Just as if, monks, when a carpenter or carpenter's apprentice looks upon his adze-handle and sees thereon his thumb-mark and his finger-marks he does not thereby know: "So and so much of my adze-handle has been worn away today, so much yesterday, so much at other times." But he knows the wearing away of it just by its wearing away.*

Evenso some of the wrong view is eliminated each time there is mindfulness of nāma or rūpa, but we cannot see how much is eliminated each day.

Question: But when there is strong attachment or when we are very angry how can there be awareness at the same time?

Nina: When there is a lobha-mūla-citta (citta rooted in attachment) or a dosa-mūla-citta (citta rooted in ill-will), there cannot be a citta with mindfulness at the same time, since there can only be one citta at a time. But shortly after the akusala citta has fallen away there can be kusala citta with mindfulness. The characteristic of akusala can then be the object of mindfulness, and it can be known as nāma, not self.

Question: Can we not be so disturbed by lobha or dosa, especially when they are intense, that awareness is impossible?

Nina: Are strong desire and intense anger realities?

Question: Yes, they appear, they are realities.

Nina: Then they can be known as they are. If one makes oneself believe that it is impossible to be aware of particular realities, one has not understood what the eightfold Path is: the development of right understanding of whatever reality appears. Some people are so afraid of akusala citta that they try to flee from the reality which appears at that moment. They think that they should apply themselves to a particular practice, such as concentrating on their breathing, in order to regulate awareness. When they act in this way without awareness of the reality which appears at the present moment, they are not developing the eightfold Path. When one develops the eightfold Path which is called the "middle way", there should be awareness of any kind of reality which appears, even if it is akusala.

We may be inclined to think that there should not be mindfulness of akusala cittas, especially of those types we find particularly ugly such as cittas with strong desire or anger. Why should we be worried by the reality which appears, even if it is akusala citta? We cannot change the reality which has already appeared, but we can know its characteristic. It is useless to go on worrying about strong desire or anger. At such moments there are nāma and rūpa. Why would it not be possible to know these realities as they are: only conditioned phenomena which are not self?

Through vipassanā we come to know more our akusala cittas, not only the coarse ones but also the more subtle ones. Not only strong desire is lobha, but also enjoyment of beautiful things is lobha. We cannot force ourselves not to enjoy beautiful things since we have accumulated attachment, but we should know that at such moments the cittas are not kusala cittas but akusala cittas. The "middle way" is not forcing oneself to particular practices in order to suppress attachment, but it is knowing whatever reality appears. We should also know moha-mūla-cittas (cittas rooted in ignorance) as they are. Most of the time we do not realize when there are moha-mūla-cittas because moha-mūla-citta is not accompanied by pleasant feeling or by unpleasant feeling, but by indifferent feeling. We may not realize that when the feeling is indifferent there can be akusala citta. When there are no kusala cittas, there are not only many moments of lobha-mūla-citta and dosa-mūla-citta, but also of moha-mūla-citta. We are often ignorant of the nāmas and rūpas which appear, there are countless moments of forgetfulness and ignorance. Moha is dangerous. The moha of today conditions moha in the future. How many more lives will we be ignorant of realities? Through the development of vipassanā we will realize that we are still ignorant of many realities.

Question: I thought that the Buddha said that one should be aware every time one is breathing in and breathing out. Should we not concentrate on breathing?

Nina: So long as we are breathing there is still life. All through life mindfulness should be developed. In vipassanā one does not select any particular object of mindfulness. There can be mindfulness of whatever kind of nāma or rūpa appears through one of the six doors; in this way wrong view and doubt about the realities one takes for "self" can be eradicated.

In vipassanā one does not have to follow any rule. One does not have to concentrate on breathing; if one selects the object of awareness and in this way tries to control sati, there will not be detachment from the wrong view of self. When we speak of breathing, we are using a conventional term of every day language. What are the realities which can be directly experienced when breathing? There can be awareness of phenomena such as softness, hardness, heat, cold, motion or pressure when they present themselves through the door of the bodysense, and they can be known as different kinds of rūpa. Nāmas and rūpas appear, but there is no self who can decide of which reality there should be awareness.

Question: Reflecting on what you said about awareness of nāma and rūpa, I can accept and understand that there is no self, but I cannot experience it as the truth. And sometimes I still feel that there must be a self who directs the mind and makes decisions. Suppose that I decide today to study the teachings and to observe the five precepts; I find it difficult to believe that there is not an ego or self who makes this choice, this decision.

Nina: So long as we are not ariyans, the wrong view of self has not been eradicated; there are yet conditions for clinging to the concept of self. Awareness of nāmas and rūpas will gradually lead to a clearer understanding of what things really are. Then we shall realize that decision-making is a type of nāma arising because of conditions. When wisdom has been developed to the degree that enlightenment can be attained there will be no more doubt about realities and there will be the clear comprehension that there is no self.

In order to develop the right Path there must be from the beginning right understanding about the way of development. If there is some misunderstanding in the beginning one may go the wrong way for a long time. It may be very hard to find the right way again. If one continues having wrong understanding, for how many more lives will there be wrong view?

Question: Is the development of the right Path just watching or observing all the phenomena of one's life?

Nina: Who is watching? There may be an idea of self who is watching and one may not notice this.

The development of right understanding is not watching or observing. When visible object appears it can be known as only a reality which is experienced through the eyesense, not somebody, not something. When seeing appears it can be known as only the experience of visible object, no self who sees. When one pays attention to the shape and form of something there is another type of nāma, different from seeing, and its characteristic can be known too. All realities which appear through the six doors can be object of mindfulness. Mindfulness is not self, it arises because it is conditioned by listening to the Dhamma, by the study of the Dhamma and by right consideration of it. From the beginning there should not be an idea of self who is watching phenomena or who can select the object of mindfulness.

A very precise knowledge of all the different phenomena which appear should be developed in order to see them as they are, as anattā, beyond control. This is the development of the eightfold Path.

Chapter 14

Factors of the Eightfold Path

Questioner: It is important to cultivate wholesomeness, not only in our actions and speech but in our thinking as well. It is, however, impossible to think wholesome thoughts all the time because we have accumulated many defilements. When we think of the virtues of the Buddha there are at those moments wholesome thoughts, but we cannot continually think of wholesome things; we cannot help it that unwholesome thoughts arise many times during the day. How can we stop unwholesome thinking?

Nina: When we recollect the Buddha's virtues and when we are grateful for the Dhamma he taught out of compassion for the world, it is a condition for wholesome thinking. We could visit the four holy places: the place of the Buddha's birth, of his enlightenment, of his first sermon and of his final passing away. In visiting those holy places we give expression to our deep confidence in his teachings and our gratefulness for the Dhamma which even after 2500 years can still help us now, at this very moment. The holy places remind us not to be neglectful of mindfulness; they are conditions for many kusala cittas.

When there are kusala cittas there are at those moments no conditions for unwholesome thinking, but it is not eradicated. Only by the cultivation of the eightfold Path, which is the development of insight, will unwholesome thinking eventually be eradicated. In the development of vipassanā there can also be mindfulness of thinking which is unwholesome. We may not like to be mindful of unwholesome thinking, but it is a reality, it arises, and thus its characteristic can be investigated. The Four Applications of Mindfulness or satipaṭṭhāna include all realities. If we understand that there isn't anything which cannot be object of mindfulness, we will gradually realize that all phenomena are only nāma and rūpa. Thus, when unwholesome thinking appears why can it not be known as only a type of nāma? When paññā knows the characteristic of this reality more clearly, there will be less inclination to take it for self. So long as we are not yet arahats unwholesomeness is bound to arise. It can only be completely eradicated when one has attained arahatship.

Question: I learned that "right thinking" or "sammā-saṇkappa" is one of the factors of the eightfold Path. Is sammā-saṇkappa thinking of nāma and rūpa?

Nina: Sammā-saṇkappa is the cetasika, mental factor, which is "vitakka" or "thinking". Vitakka is usually translated into English as "applied thought". The characteristic of vitakka is different from what we mean by the word "thinking" as we use it in conventional language. Vitakka performs a specific function when it accompanies the citta. The *Visuddhimagga*(IV, 88) states about vitakka:

> *...It has the characteristic of directing the mind onto an object (mounting the mind on its object). Its function is to strike and thresh... It is manifested as the leading of the mind onto an object.*

Vitakka accompanies many cittas but not every citta. It arises together with the citta and falls away with the citta. When vitakka accompanies akusala citta it is also akusala, and when it accompanies kusala citta it is also kusala. When vitakka accompanies the citta with right understanding (sammā-diṭṭhi) and right mindfulness (sammā-sati) of the eightfold Path it is called *sammā-saṇkappa, right thinking,* of the eightfold Path. When there is right mindfulness of a nāma or rūpa which appears through one of the six doors, sammā-saṇkappa hits or "touches" the nāma or rūpa which is the object of mindfulness so that sammā-diṭṭhi can investigate that object in order to know it as it is. When right understanding has not been developed yet, we may doubt whether the reality which appears is nāma or rūpa. When there is seeing which is nāma there is also visible object which is rūpa, but only one reality at a time can be object of mindfulness. It is the function of sammā-saṇkappa to "touch" the reality appearing at the present moment so that right understanding can investigate its characteristic. Right understanding needs right thinking in order to investigate the characteristics of nāma and rūpa and to see realities as they are. Thus, sammā-saṇkappa is indispensable for the development of right understanding. If we understand the function of sammā-saṇkappa, it is clear that sammā-saṇkappa is not thinking about nāma or rūpa.

Question: Can sammā-saṇkappa destroy wrong thinking?

Nina: Sammā-saṇkappa arises together with the citta which is accompanied by right mindfulness and right understanding. It directs the citta in the right way towards the object of mindfulness and at that moment there cannot be wrong thinking. After the moment of mindfulness, however, wrong thinking or thinking which is akusala can arise again, but if one continues developing the eightfold Path it will eventually be destroyed.

Question: I heard someone say that in order to develop mindfulness one should stop thinking. Is this a right method?

Nina: How could we prevent ourselves from thinking? Throughout our life objects are presenting themselves through the senses and through the mind-door. Cittas which think of these objects are real. Why can there not be mindfulness of thinking? Otherwise we will not see that it is anattā, not self. The moment we try to control thinking it has fallen away, it already belongs to the past. When there is awareness of a characteristic of nāma or rūpa, there is at that moment no clinging to a concept of self who tries to stop thinking or to control sati in other ways. Awareness of whatever reality appears, that is the development of the eightfold Path.

Question: We have spoken already about sammā-diṭṭhi, sammā-saṇkappa and sammā-sati, but there are eight factors of the eightfold Path. Could you tell me which are the factors of the eightfold Path?

Nina: The eight factors are:

Right understanding, sammā-diṭṭhi
Right thinking, sammā-saṇkappa
Right speech, sammā-vācā
Right bodily action, sammā-kammanta
Right livelihood, sammā-ājīva
Right effort, sammā-vāyāma
Right mindfulness, sammā-sati
Right concentration, sammā-samādhi

Question: What are the functions of right speech, right bodily action and right livelihood?

Nina: They are three sobhana cetasikas, beautiful mental factors, which abstain from wrong speech, wrong bodily action and wrong livelihood. They are the factors which are sīla or morality. Right speech is abstaining from wrong speech, which is lying, slandering, rude speech and idle talk. Right action is abstaining from wrong bodily action, which is killing, stealing and sexual misbehaviour. Right livelihood is abstaining from wrong livelihood, which is wrong bodily action and wrong speech committed for the sake of earning a living.

Question: How can I abstain from wrong speech? I find that when I am with other people who speak in an unwholesome way I am inclined to do the same.

Nina: So long as we are not yet arahats we will still speak in an unwholesome way. But the Buddha's teachings can be the condition for us to have less akusala in our life. When people speak in an unpleasant way about others or when they complain about disagreeable things which happen in life we may be inclined to follow their example. But through the study of the teachings and the development of satipaṭṭhāna we will realize more often when there are akusala cittas. Gradually we can learn to abstain from wrong speech. We may have compassion for those who speak in the wrong way, we may try to help them to have kusala cittas instead of akusala cittas.

Question: We may know this in theory, but I find the practice of the teachings very difficult. I have spoken the wrong words already before I realize it.

Nina: Through the development of right understanding habits and accumulations can gradually be changed. But there is no self who could change habits and accumulations. The right understanding of the Dhamma and the application of the Dhamma in one's life are conditions for change. Then we can prove to ourselves that the Buddha's teachings are the truth; and our confidence in the teachings will be deeper.

Question: Can you give an example of right action?

Nina: When we are inclined to kill an insect which is stinging us, but then, instead of having aversion, we abstain from killing, we are observing sīla. It is not self who abstains, but the cetasika which is right action performs its function.

Question: I know of someone who says that he cannot help killing. When an insect bites him it is his reflex to kill it. Is the development of right understanding a condition for abstaining from wrong action?

Nina: Right understanding of nāma and rūpa conditions us to realize more often the danger of akusala and the benefit of kusala. At the moment of mindfulness of a reality which appears through one of the six doors there is kusala citta. Kusala citta cannot be accompanied by dosa, it is accompanied by adosa. Adosa is non-aversion or lovingkindness. Right understanding can gradually be the condition that kindness and compassion arise more often. We will be more inclined to think of the happiness of other beings. Should we cause insects to have pain, should we destroy their lives?

Question: When one develops right understanding of the eightfold Path do the sobhana cetasikas of right action, right speech and right livelihood destroy wrong action, wrong speech and wrong livelihood?

Nina: The development of right understanding is a condition for more wholesomeness in our life, but akusala cannot be eradicated immediately. There are at times conditions for abstaining from unwholesome actions and unwholesome speech, but, when enlightenment has not been attained sīla is not enduring. When we are in difficult situations we may kill and we may lie. The sotāpanna, the person who has attained the first stage of enlightenment has no more conditions for committing akusala kamma which can cause an unhappy rebirth. He has no more conditions to transgress the five precepts. However, he has not eradicated all kinds of unwholesomeness. He has eradicated wrong bodily action, and as regards wrong speech, he has eradicated lying, but he has not eradicated the other kinds of wrong speech. He has eradicated wrong livelihood, he cannot commit wrong action or wrong speech for the sake of earning a living. Thus we see that the development of right understanding will bear directly on our action and speech in daily life.

When the citta is not lokuttara citta, supramundane citta which experiences nibbāna, the three factors of right speech, right action and right livelihood arise one at a time, depending on the given situation. When we abstain from wrong action, we do not abstain at the same time from wrong speech. At the attainment of enlightenment, however, all three factors arise together while they accompany the lokuttara citta which experiences nibbāna. They perform at that moment their functions as Path factors which is the eradication of the causes of misconduct as to speech, action and livelihood. Latent tendencies to defilements are eradicated so that they do not arise anymore. Defilements are progressively eradicated at the different stages of enlightenment and it is only at the final stage, the stage of the arahat, that all kinds of akusala are completely eradicated.

Question: Can there be awareness of nāma and rūpa while we abstain from unwholesomeness?

Nina: There can be the development of right understanding in any situation, no matter whether we have akusala cittas or whether we abstain from akusala. We gradually learn that there is no self who has kusala citta or akusala citta, but that these types of citta arise because of their own conditions. Through the development of right understanding sīla will become purer because one will realize that it is not self who observes sīla.

Question: So long as one has not become a sotāpanna the observing of the five precepts which include abstaining from wrong bodily action and from lying cannot be enduring. There will be situations that one will transgress them. As regards wrong livelihood, for some people it is very difficult to abstain from it. I heard of someone who has no choice but to kill chickens in order to earn a living for his family. Every day he has to kill, but he says that he performs dāna, generosity, in order to compensate for his killing. Can he compensate in that way?

Nina: We cannot compensate for bad actions by good actions, because every deed brings about its appropriate result. The killing, which is akusala kamma, may cause an unhappy rebirth, even if we perform good deeds as well.

Question: But this person cannot earn a living in any other way. He used to have another kind of business but he could not earn enough money to take care of his family. Some people have no choice; they have to do wrong actions for their livelihood.

Nina: Nothing in life happens without conditions. One's accumulated defilements cause one to have a profession by which one is involved in killing animals or trading in arms or alcoholic drinks. These professions are wrong livelihood; they are conditions for akusala kamma. It is sati which could, one day, make a person change his profession which is wrong livelihood. People may think that it is impossible to change their profession, but if there is the development of right understanding of realities there will be conditions for earning one's living without having to perform akusala kamma. As we have seen, the sotāpanna has completely eradicated the tendency to wrong livelihood.

Question: What about people who are not trading in the things you just mentioned, but who are what we call "in business"? I would think that if one is to make a profit one cannot always be telling the truth. Should business-men change their profession in order to be pure in their livelihood? I know someone who was formerly in business but changed his profession. He now works for a newspaper because he sees this profession as an opportunity to serve other people better.

Nina: We cannot say that someone should or should not do particular things, because whatever we do in life is dependent on conditions. There is no self who makes a choice, there are cittas arising because of their own conditions. People who are in business may perform akusala kamma, as for instance, when they are dishonest and harm other people in the way they make their profit. But they can have kusala cittas too. They may abstain from telling lies even though they know that this will cause them to have less profit. Thus, at different moments there are different conditions for akusala cittas and for kusala cittas which arise.

Question: What about a professional soldier? Can he ever have right livelihood?

Nina: He can have akusala cittas and kusala cittas at different moments. When he kills others he performs akusala kamma, but he may also perform wholesome deeds.

In the *Sutta of the Highest Blessings*(Mahā-Maṅgala Sutta, Sutta-Nipāta, Khuddaka Nikāya) we read among others about the following blessing: "Supporting mother and father, cherishing wife and children, and peaceful occupations—this is the highest blessing."

Soldiers, however, can and should cultivate kusala kamma too. We read in the *Gradual Sayings* (Book of the Eights, Ch II, § 2,

Sīha, the general)) that Sīha the general visited the Buddha and gained confidence in him. We read:

> *Then the Exalted One preached a graduated discourse to Sīha, the general, that is to say: on almsgiving, the precepts and on heaven. He set forth the peril, the folly and the depravity of lusts and the blessedness of renunciation.*
>
> *And when the Exalted One knew that the heart of Sīha, the general, was clear, malleable, free from hindrance, uplifted and lucid, then he revealed that teaching of Dhamma which Buddhas alone have won, that is to say: Dukkha, its coming-to-be, its ending and the Way. Just as a clean cloth, free of all stain, will take dye perfectly; even so in Sīha, the general, seated there, there arose the spotless, stainless vision of Dhamma: that whatsoever be conditioned by coming-to-be all that is subject to ending...*

The commentary to this sutta, the "Manorathapūraṇi", explains that Sīha became a sotāpanna.

Question: I think that those whose profession is government service have more conditions for pure livelihood. They do not have to think about making a profit for themselves.

Nina: They may have many akusala cittas; they may have conceit, or they may think of their own success. It all depends on the individual. When we have chosen a profession, it shows that we have accumulations for that profession. That profession is part of our daily life. During our work we can develop mindfulness and right understanding of nāma and rūpa. When we have more understanding of the Dhamma we can help other people to understand it as well, and thus we serve society in the best way, we contribute to peace in the world.

Question: But can someone who has to think of money all day be aware of nāma and rūpa?

Nina: Do you handle money during the day?

Question: Yes, it is part of our normal way of life.

Nina: Should you not be aware of realities when looking at money? Do you think that there is anything which is not included in satipaṭṭhāna?

Question: When I look at money visible object appears through the eyes. When I touch it hardness or softness may appear through the bodysense. But if I were aware only of those realities and did not know the value of the banknote I would be poor very soon. Even though I believe that awareness is very useful, yet I consider it to be a different section of life. I lead two kinds of lives: my life of awareness which I lead mostly at home, when I am alone, and my business life in which I have to be practical.

Nina: Do you think that the Buddha said that there are times one should not be mindful? He exhorted people to be aware, no matter what they were doing.

Question: But awareness is not always practical. For instance, when I am opening the safe in my office I have to remember the numbers of the combination-lock. If I were aware only of hardness, motion or visible object, I could not open the safe. I thought that only absolute realities, nāmas and rūpas which appear one at a time through the six doors are objects of mindfulness. I thought that there cannot be mindfulness while one is thinking of concepts.

Nina: Why can there not be awareness when you know the value of a banknote or when you remember the numbers of the combination-lock on the safe? At such moments there is thinking of concepts, but is thinking not a reality? Are there moments that there are not nāma and rūpa? I agree that you have to be practical, but does that mean that there cannot be awareness at the same time?

The Buddha's teachings are very practical. The Buddha gave many practical guidelines for laypeople so that they could lead a life of goodwill and benevolence in their social relations. He advised them on the means for both their material welfare and their spiritual welfare. We read in the *Gradual Sayings* (Book of the Eights, Ch VI, § 4, Longknee, the Koḷiyan) that, while the Buddha was staying among the Koḷiyans, at Kakkarapatta, Longknee (also named "Tigerfoot") visited the Buddha. He asked the Buddha whether he would teach Dhamma to people like him, who are householders indulging in sense pleasures. He would like the Buddha to teach him what would lead to happiness here on earth and to happiness in the world to come. The Buddha said that four conditions would lead to advantage and happiness here on earth, namely, alertness, achievement in watchfulness, good company and the "even life". As to alertness, he should be deft and tireless in his work, he should have an inquiring turn of mind into ways and means, and be able to carry out his job. As to "accomplishment of watchfulness"[1], we read:

> *What is the accomplishment of watchfulness? Herein, Tigerfoot (Vyagghapajja), whatsoever wealth a householder is in possession of, obtained by dint of effort, collected by strength of arm, by the sweat of his brow, justly acquired by right means–such he looks after well by guarding and watching so that kings would not seize it, thieves would not steal it, fire would not burn it, water would not carry it away, nor ill-disposed heirs would remove it. This is the accomplishment of watchfulness...*

As to good company, the Buddha said that he should consort with those who are full of faith, virtue, charity and wisdom, and try to be likewise. As to the "even life", we read:

> *... Herein a clansman while experiencing both gain and loss in wealth, continues his business serenely, not unduly elated or depressed. He thinks: "Thus my income, after deducting loss, will stand (at so much) and my outgoings will not exceed my income"...*

We read that there are four channels for the flowing away of amassed wealth: "looseness with women, debauchery in drinking, knavery in dice-play and friendship, companionship and intimacy with evil doers." The Buddha explained that there are four conditions for happiness in the world to come: achievement in faith, namely, confidence in the Buddha, achievement in virtue, that is, abstaining from ill deeds, achievement in generosity and achievement in wisdom.

The Buddha would not teach anything which is not practical and beneficial. There should be awareness not only of realities which appear through the five sense-doors, but also of realities which appear through the mind-door. When we are thinking of concepts, there can be awareness of thinking. Can you help knowing the value of a banknote? Is knowing this a reality?

Question: Yes, it is a reality.

Nina: Anything which is real can be object of mindfulness.

[1] Here I use the translation of the Wheel Publication no. 14, Buddhist Publication Society, Sri Lanka.

Some people think that there should be awareness only of some particular kinds of nāma and rūpa, such as seeing and visible object. They think that knowing what something is, as for instance, knowing the value of a banknote or knowing whether the traffic light is green or red, is not included in satipaṭṭhāna. Don't you think that unnatural? I have heard of someone who, while he is developing insight, believes that he cannot recognize his friends or his parents. If one cannot recognize anything while one is "mindful" it means that one could not be aware during one's daily activities. It means that if one were to drive a car and be "mindful" at the same time, one would not know when the traffic light is green and when it is red. That is not the right path. Recognizing something is a reality as well, it is a type of nāma which recognizes something, it is not self who recognizes. The development of the eightfold Path is the development of right understanding of all realities of our daily life.

Question: I still do not see how one can lead one's daily life while one develops vipassanā. I have heard that it is forbidden to take alcoholic drinks while one develops vipassanā.

Nina: No one can force another person to abstain from drinking, nor can one force oneself, since it is not self who indulges in drinking or abstains from it, but nāma, arising because of conditions. It is not self but sati which keeps someone from drinking. When sati has been accumulated more it is a condition for gradually becoming less attached to drinking. However, only the ariyan can observe the five precepts perfectly. Since at the attainment of enlightenment all tendencies to wrong bodily action and to the wrong speech which is lying were eradicated, it has become his nature to observe the five precepts. People who are not ariyans may transgress them. For example, when there are conditions it could happen that we kill in order to protect our lives. However, if one learns to develop satipaṭṭhāna, it will gradually lead to changing one's way of life and to refraining from akusala kamma.

Question: Thus, mindfulness can bring about what I would consider a miracle, a transformation in character, is that right?

Nina: People would like to change their characters but they do not know how to do it. Would you like to see a change in your character for the better? Is there a way? Everything occurs because of conditions. The condition for a change in one's life is vipassanā, the right understanding of realities. However, a sudden transformation of character cannot be expected. People can see for themselves that while they develop the eightfold Path they come to know more and more their defilements, also the subtle ones. When there is less ignorance of the realities of one's life it means that there is already a gradual change in one's character, even though enlightenment has not been attained.

Chapter 15

Right Effort

Questioner: Awareness arises when there are conditions. We cannot make awareness arise at will; awareness is anattā. It would seem, therefore, that we cannot make an effort to have awareness. I know, however, that right effort, in Pāli: sammā-vāyāma, is one of the factors of the eightfold Path. What is the characteristic of right effort?

Nina: Sammā-vāyāma or right effort is the cetasika which is effort or energy, in Pāli: viriya. The *Visuddhimagga* (XIV, 137) states about viriya:

> *Energy (viriya) is the state of one who is vigorous (vīra). Its characteristic is marshalling (driving). Its function is to consolidate conascent states. It is manifested as non-collapse. Because of the words "Bestirred, he strives wisely" (Anguttara Nikāya II, 115[1]) its proximate cause is a sense of urgency; or its proximate cause is grounds for the initiation of energy. When rightly initiated, it should be regarded as the root of all attainments.*

Viriya is a type of nāma but is it not true that we take it for self? There are different kinds of viriya. There is viriya which is akusala and there is viriya which is kusala. There is viriya with dāna, viriya with sīla, viriya in samatha and viriya in vipassanā, which is right effort of the eightfold Path (sammā-vāyāma), and all these kinds of viriya have different qualities.

Sammā-vāyāma of the eightfold Path arises together with sammā-diṭṭhi, right understanding and sammā-sati, right mindfulness. The development of vipassanā is not merely being mindful of

[1] Book of the Fours, Ch XII, § 3, The goad. The Buddha uses a simile of horses which are stirred by a goad. Evenso a person may be stirred to develop right understanding. Some people are already stirred when they hear about someone else who is ill or dead, while others are stirred when they see it themselves, or when their own relatives are ill or dead, or when they themselves suffer from painful feelings.

realities, without investigating their characteristics. The characteristics of nāma and rūpa must be thoroughly investigated over and over again until they are understood as only a nāma or only a rūpa, non-self. Sammā-vāyāma is an indispensable factor for the development of right understanding, because much courage and perseverance are needed for the investigation of realities in order see them as they are. Sammā-vāyāma is the strength and vigour which arises each moment when there is awareness of a nāma or a rūpa and understanding of the reality which appears is being developed.

Question: You said that when sammā-diṭṭhi investigates a characteristic of nāma or rūpa which is object of mindfulness there is also sammā-vāyāma at that moment. But when there is very little awareness should we not make an effort to have more?

Nina: One may try to force the arising of awareness and try to "catch" the reality of the present moment, but then one does not know what sati is. Someone may take his attachment to sati for sati. It is true that right awareness can be developed, but this does not mean that one can force its arising. The factor which can condition its arising is understanding how vipassanā is to be developed. If we know what the object of sati is: the nāma or rūpa which appears now, through one of the six doors, sati can arise and thus right understanding can gradually develop. When a citta with right mindfulness arises, there is at that moment right effort as well. Effort in vipassanā is the strength or energy which is needed to investigate the reality which appears in order to understand it as it is, but we should remember that this effort is not self. Right effort of the eightfold Path supports and strengthens right mindfulness and right understanding.

Question: I have heard that the right effort of the eightfold Path is the effort of the "middle way". However, it is very difficult to walk the middle way. If we make too much of an effort there is the notion of self again and if we make no effort at all we are lazy and heedless. I do not know how to walk the right way.

Nina: If we think in terms of making too much or too little effort, then we do not realize that effort is nāma and not self. We should not confuse sammā-vāyāma of the eightfold Path with what we in conventional language usually mean by "effort" or "trying". We do not have to think of making an effort, because when there is right mindfulness there is at that moment sammā-vāyāma as well. Sammā-vāyāma arises for example when there is right mindfulness of seeing, hearing, thinking, visible object or sound which appears now. At such a moment there is courage and strength to be mindful of the reality which appears in order to develop a clearer understanding of its characteristic.

Question: When sati does not arise we cannot force its arising. Does this mean that nothing else can be done but waiting for the arising of sati?

Nina: We should not waste our life and spend it in heedlessness. Thus, we should not neglect any way of kusala for which there is an opportunity. Dāna, sīla, samatha and vipassanā are different ways of kusala we can apply ourselves to. When sati of vipassanā does not arise, we should not be lazy with regard to the other ways of kusala, because at the moments we do not develop kusala, we act, speak and think with akusala cittas and thus we accumulate akusala time and again.

We should not neglect the way of kusala which is studying and considering the teachings. If we study the teachings and often consider what the Buddha taught about nāma and rūpa there are conditions for the arising of sati at any moment.

Question: When there are akusala cittas an effort should be made for kusala cittas. The person who develops samatha and the person who develops vipassanā will make an effort for kusala in different ways. Is that right?

Nina: Samatha is the development of calm by means of a suitable meditation subject. The kusala citta which applies itself to samatha is accompanied by right effort, sammā-vāyāma, but this kind of effort is different from sammā-vāyāma of the eightfold Path. Sammā-vāyāma in samatha supports the citta which develops calm in order to temporarily eliminate akusala cittas. Sammā-vāyāma of the eightfold Path supports the citta and the accompanying mental factors, when there is right mindfulness of whatever reality appears, in order that it will be known as it is, as non-self. When there is akusala citta, it can be realised as a type of nāma, arising because of conditions, not self.

It is important to know what one is developing, samatha or vipassanā. When people say that they develop vipassanā but do not want to be aware of akusala cittas, they are not on the eightfold

Path. Most people are afraid of gross defilements, but does one realize the danger of latent tendencies which have been accumulated? Latent tendencies are dangerous; they are a condition for akusala cittas to arise; they are the condition for us to be born again and again. Vipassanā is the only way to eradicate all defilements and also the latent tendencies. Therefore, vipassanā is the highest way of kusala.

Question: Are there many moments of mindfulness needed before there can be a clear understanding of realities?

Nina: In the beginning there cannot be a clear understanding of nāma and rūpa. We often mention the words nāma and rūpa but we should keep in mind that these words denote *realities* which can be known through direct experience in our daily life. Seeing, hearing or thinking are nâmas which can be directly known when they appear. Visible object, sound or hardness are rūpas which can be directly known when they appear. We still think of a self who sees, hears or thinks, but what we take for a person are in fact many different elements which can be known one at a time. Hearing is only an element, a type of nāma which experiences sound. Hearing cannot experience any other object. Through mindfulness of hearing when it appears we will learn that not a self hears, but that hearing hears. When sound appears sound can be the object of mindfulness; there is at that moment no thought of the sound of a voice or the sound of a particular thing. When there is mindfulness of sound, its characteristic can be investigated and this is the way to know sound as it is: a rūpa which is experienced through the ears, not a thing which belongs to a person, not a "self". Most of the time there is forgetfulness of realities. At the moment sati arises there is mindfulness of one reality at a time, a nāma-element or a rūpa-element.

Right understanding of nāma and rūpa can only develop at the moment there is mindfulness of their characteristics as they appear through the six doorways. Each moment of developing right understanding is extremely short, it arises and then falls away immediately. In the beginning there will be only be a few moments of sati and then there are bound to be countless moments of forgetfulness of realities. Many moments of sati are needed in order that the characteristics of nāma and rūpa can be investigated, but this should not make us discouraged. A moment of right mindfulness is never lost, it conditions mindfulness again, later on. It is inpredictable when sati will arise, because it is anattā, non-self. The development of satipaṭṭhāna is the only way to have less ignorance of realities. If we really see the danger of ignorance it can be a condition for the arising of sati and then there is right effort as well.

It is important to know the difference between thinking about nāma and rūpa and the paññā which directly knows the characteristic of the nāma or rūpa which appears. We may think that we know nāma and rūpa from direct experience, but is there a clear understanding of their different characteristics? Do we know already through direct experience the difference between the characteristic of nāma and the characteristic of rūpa? We have learned that nāma is the reality which experiences something and that rūpa is the reality which does not know anything, but now we should know their different characteristics through the direct experience, in being mindful of them. So long as there is doubt about the difference between nāma and rūpa, there cannot be a clear understanding of them.

Question: I think that I can experience the impermanence of seeing. I know that it has fallen away when other phenomena appear. When, for instance, there is hearing it is clear that seeing has fallen away.

Nina: Knowing impermanence by way of thinking is not the same as the direct understanding of the arising and falling away of realities. It is difficult to realize this. During the time we call in conventional language a "moment" there are countless cittas arising and falling away, succeeding one another. If one has not cultivated right understanding to a high degree the impermanence of cittas cannot be realized.

Question: I see that it is important to know impermanence through direct experience in order to eliminate wrong understanding of realities. How can I ever be quick enough to know the impermanence of cittas?

Nina: This can never be known so long as there a concept of self who tries to take hold of realities. Only paññā can realize the nāma or rūpa appearing at the present moment.

Question: What can be known by direct experience when one has only just begun to develop insight?

Nina: There can be mindfulness of a characteristic which appears through one of the six doors. But there cannot yet be a precise knowledge of nāma and rūpa. Someone told me that he assumed that everybody knew the difference between nāma and rūpa; for example, between the nāma which experiences sound, hearing, and the rūpa which is sound. He was wondering how anybody could have doubts about it. However, we should know the difference between theoretical knowledge and the paññā which has direct understanding of realities. Only when paññā has been developed in vipassanā can it have a precise knowledge of the reality which appears at the present moment.

Question: There are many phenomena arising at the same time. In what order should I be aware of phenomena?

Nina: It is true that there are many phenomena arising at the same time. For example, our body consists of many different rūpas which arise and fall away. The rūpas which are solidity, cohesion, temperature and motion always arise together and fall away together. But only one characteristic can be experienced by citta at a time, because citta can have only one object at a time. Thus, when the citta is accompanied by sammā-sati, right mindfulness, there can be mindfulness of only one reality at a time. When we say that hardness appears or presents itself it means that hardness is the object which citta experiences at that moment. If sati accompanies the citta, then sati has the same object as the citta; it is mindful of that object. When there is mindfulness of the characteristic of hardness, paññā can realize it as only hardness; it is not a body, not a self, it is only a kind of rūpa which is experienced through the door of the body. It is beyond control what the object of awareness will be. There is no rule which tells us of which phenomena there should be awareness and in which order.

Direct understanding of realities by being mindful of them is not the same as theoretical knowledge of them, but theoretical knowledge of nāma and rūpa is a helpful foundation for the development of vipassanā. When we read the suttas we notice that the Buddha spoke time and again about understanding nāma and rūpa which appear through the six doorways. We read for example in the *Kindred Sayings* (IV, Saḷāyatana-vagga, Kindred Sayings on Sense, Third Fifty, Ch V, § 146, Helpful) that the

Buddha said to the monks:

> *I will teach you, monks, a way that is helpful for nibbāna. Do you listen to it. And what, monks, is that way? Herein, monks, a monk regards the eye as impermanent. He regards objects, eye-consciousness, eye-contact as impermanent. That pleasant, unpleasant or neutral feeling experienced, which arises by eye-contact–that also he regards as impermanent.*
>
> *He regards the ear... the nose... the tongue... the body... He regards mind, mind-states, mind-consciousness, mind-contact as impermanent. The pleasant feeling or unpleasant feeling or neutral feeling... arising therefrom,— he regards that also as impermanent.*
>
> *This, monks, is the way that is helpful for nibbāna.*

Would thinking about realities as impermanent lead to nibbāna? We cannot become detached from the concept of self merely by thinking. Only the paññā which directly understands the characteristics of nāma and rūpa which appear at the present moment can see them as they really are, as impermanent and non-self.

If we mistakenly think that we know the truth already we are not able to understand the real meaning of this sutta. Why would the Buddha time and again stress that the eye, seeing-consciousness and visible object, that all realities appearing through the six doors are impermanent? In order to remind people to be aware of nāma and rūpa, so that one day they would see realities as they are.

Question: I find it difficult to know from direct experience the difference between the nāma which experiences sound and the rūpa which is sound. How can I ever know the difference between nāma and rūpa unless I make an effort? Or would it be better in the beginning to ignore the difference between nāma and rūpa, such as hearing and sound, and rather know different characteristics of rūpa which appear through the bodysense?

Nina: All nāmas and rūpas which appear through the different doorways should be known. We should not select any particular kind of nāma or rūpa as object of awareness. That would not be the right path. Hearing can be known and sound can be known as well, they are both realities which each have a different characteristic. We cannot, however, have a clear understanding of realities within just a short time. The characteristics of nāma and rūpa are clearly distinguished from each other when the first stage of insight-knowledge is attained. Even this stage, which is only a beginning stage, cannot be attained unless there has been mindfulness over and over again of nāma and rūpa. Could we say that we know already different kinds of nāma and rūpa as they appear through the different doorways? Are we no longer confused as to the doorway through which an object is experienced?

Question: No, I certainly cannot say that.

Nina: How could there be a precise knowledge of realities when their characteristics are not yet known from direct experience, as they appear one at a time through eyes, ears, nose, tongue, bodysense and mind-door? All these considerations help us to realize how little we know. If we wrongly assume that we know realities as they are we cannot develop right understanding. But when we see how little we know we are more truthful and then we may be able to begin to develop right understanding.

When right understanding develops we begin to realize the difference between theoretical knowledge of realities and the paññā which directly knows the characteristics of phenomena when they appear one at a time. We realize that a few moments of awareness are not enough; that we need to be mindful of nāma and rūpa countless times in order to become more familiar with their characteristics. In that way a more precise knowledge of nāma and rūpa can be developed.

Question: In the *Visuddhimagga*, in the definition of effort, it is said that its proximate cause is "a sense of urgency" or "grounds for the initiation of energy". What can urge us to be mindful now?

Nina: The Buddha pointed out that it is a matter of urgency for us to develop right understanding of realities; he encouraged people to be mindful, at any time and any place. He pointed out the sorrows of past lives, of the present life and of the lives in the future which will occur if one has not made an end to rebirth.

In the *Theragātha* (Vajjita, Canto II, 168) we read about Vajjita who attained arahatship. The text states:

A traveller I these long, long ages past,
And round about the realms of life I've whirled;
One of the many-folk and blind as they,

No ariyan truths had I the power to see.
But earnestly I strove for light and calm;
And now all shattered lies the endless way.
All future bournes abolished utterly,
Now comes never more rebirth for me.

We do not know how long we will be in this plane of existence nor whether we will be able to develop insight in the next life. When we read in the scriptures about birth, old age, sickness and death, and about the dangers of rebirth, we can be reminded to be aware of realities now, at this moment. When we see that mindfulness now is urgent and that it should not be put off, it can help us to be less neglectful.

Sammā-vāyāma, right effort, is an indispensable factor of the eightfold Path; it supports and strengthens right understanding and right mindfulness. One needs vigour and courage to be mindful without delay and to consider and investigate the characteristics of nāma and rūpa untiringly, so that right understanding can grow. Realities such as seeing, visible object, hearing, sound, feeling or thinking appear countless times during the day, yet often there is no mindfulness but forgetfulness of realities. If there is no mindfulness now, will there ever be the wisdom which sees things as they are?

Question: You say that thinking about the dangers of rebirth will remind people not to be heedless. I doubt whether it is helpful to be frightened by the thought of hell.

Nina: All of the Buddha's teachings are most valuable. That is why we should continue reading the scriptures. For different situations in life we will find in the teachings the right words which will encourage us to be mindful. Often we are heedless and forgetful of realities, but when we read about the danger of rebirth in hell it reminds us to continue to develop right understanding. We should not be frightened by the thought of hell–that is akusala. But we should remember that only if vipassanā is developed and enlightenment is attained will we escape the danger of an unhappy rebirth.

When we see the extent of the defilements we have accumulated and are still accumulating, we can be urged to develop right understanding now, at this moment.

Chapter 16

Right Mindfulness

Questioner: The wisdom which sees realities as they are can only develop when there is mindfulness. Is there anything we can do in order to have mindfulness of nāma and rūpa, so that later on paññā which knows them as they are will arise?

Nina: If one wants to do something in particular in order to have mindfulness, one is led by clinging and then paññā cannot develop. Some people think that right mindfulness of the eightfold Path is something other than attending to the characteristic of nāma or rūpa which appears now, in daily life. That is the wrong understanding of mindfulness. At this moment you are sitting. Is there hardness? Can you experience it?

Question: Yes, I can experience it.

Nina: Hardness is only a kind of rūpa which appears through the bodysense. We usually think of a thing or the body which is hard and we are forgetful of the *characteristic* of hardness which appears. When there is mindfulness of the characteristic of hardness which appears we do not think of a thing or of the body which is hard and at that moment paññā can investigate the reality which is hardness. In that way hardness can be known as only a kind of rūpa which appears through the bodysense, no "self". Hardness is an ultimate reality with its own unchangeable characteristic which can be directly experienced without the need to think about it or to name it "hardness" or "rūpa". Ultimate realities are different from concepts which are not real in the ultimate sense. When we think of a thing which is hard or the body which is hard, the object of thinking is a concept. The thinking itself, however, is an ultimate reality, a type of nāma. Anything which is real, nāma and rūpa, are the objects of right mindfulness and right understanding of the eightfold Path. The right understanding of ultimate realities can eventually lead to detachment from the wrong view of self. When a reality such as hardness appears, there is also a reality which experiences hardness. It is not self who experiences hardness, but a kind of nāma, different from the rūpa which is hardness. The experience of hardness is an ultimate reality with its own characteristic which can be object of mindfulness when it presents itself, and then paññā can investigate it in order to know it as it is. Thus, sati is not forgetful, but mindful of the characteristics of nāma and rūpa as they appear one at a time through the six doors. At the moment of mindfulness of a reality paññā can investigate it and in this way it will eventually be known as it is.

We may be inclined to think that we have to do something special in order to have mindfulness and that we then can "experience" nāma and rūpa as they are, but this is not so. Right understanding of what sati is and what the object of sati is, namely an ultimate reality, can condition the arising of sati and then paññā can gradually develop. In order to know what sati is and what the object of sati we have to listen to the good friend in Dhamma who can explain the development of right understanding, we have to study the Dhamma and to consider it carefully.

Sammā-sati, right mindfulness, is one of the factors of the eightfold Path and it arises together with sammā-diṭṭhi, right understanding. Sammā-sati is mindful of a characteristic of nāma or rūpa which appears and sammā-diṭṭhi realizes it as it is.

Question: But mindfulness has to be cultivated. Do we not have to do certain things and abstain from other things we are used to doing in daily life, in order to have more mindfulness?

Nina: Studying the teachings, pondering over them, learning about the right way of practice, knowing the benefit of right understanding, these are conditions for the arising of mindfulness. When we have understood that mindfulness arises because of conditions, that it is anattā, non-self, and when we have found out for ourselves that we cannot induce mindfulness, we will refrain from doing special things in order to have more mindfulness.

Question: I know what you mean. When I sit still at home and I try to be mindful, I cannot be mindful.

Nina: When there is right understanding, we realize that the aim of vipassanā is knowing ourselves, our daily life. Therefore, we do not act in a way which is unnatural to ourselves in order to have more sati. We do not force ourselves to sit still for a long time and wait for sati to arise. Is sitting still and doing nothing the natural thing for you to do?

Question: No, I usually read or write, or I stand up and walk around and do many different things.

Nina: So, if you want to know your daily life, should you force yourself to do something which is not natural to you?

Question: No, I see that I will know myself better if I do the things I have accumulations for and which I am used to doing. However, I wonder how we can know realities as they are since a moment of sati is extremely short.

Nina: A moment of sati is extremely short; it arises and falls away with the citta. Sati is impermanent and non-self. Sati arises and falls away, but it can arise again when there are conditions. Thus characteristics of nāma and rūpa can gradually be known. If people do not realize that sati arises because there are the right conditions for its arising and if they try to induce it, they will not know what sati is. In that case paññā cannot be developed.

Question: I notice that when I do good deeds mindfulness of nāma and rūpa arises more often. Are good deeds a condition for mindfulness of nāma and rūpa?

Nina: Good deeds are beneficial and they are a condition to have less akusala cittas, but we should not assume that there is necessarily more mindfulness of nāma and rūpa while we perform them. The arising of sati depends on conditions, and there is no self who can regulate its arising. We should not mistakenly believe that there cannot be awareness also of akusala cittas; after akusala citta has fallen away citta with sati may arise and then also the reality which is akusala can be object of mindfulness. The Buddha said that all kinds of realities can be known as they are. Mindfulness should not be limited to certain times, places or occasions.

Question: But is it not important for those who begin to develop mindfulness to be in a special place?

Nina: It is right understanding which is important. In vipassanā we come to know six worlds—the world appearing:

through the eyes,
through the ears,
through the nose,
through the tongue,
through the bodysense,
through the mind-door.

We should learn to distinguish between these six worlds in

order to know the truth. Only one "world" at a time is object of mindfulness. When we think of a person, an animal or a tree, there is a concept of a "whole" and we do not distinguish between these six worlds. When there is mindfulness of a reality such as visible object, which is the "world appearing through the eyes", or hardness, which is the "world appearing through the bodysense", we learn to understand the difference between thinking of concepts and mindfulness of ultimate realities as they appear one at a time. In order to develop right understanding of realities we have to know the difference. The "six worlds" are everywhere, no matter where we are; there should be mindfulness of nāma and rūpa which are those six worlds, in order to know the truth.

Question: In the beginning, when there is very little awareness, we are likely to become impatient. We think that there never will be any result. Would it not be helpful to be in a quiet place, such as a meditation centre?

Nina: When we begin to develop vipassanā we are anxious to have immediate results. We want to experience nāma and rūpa as they are and to eradicate defilements without delay. People may become tense in their effort to control awareness and thus they deviate from the right path. If they are on the wrong path they do not have right awareness and can therefore not develop right understanding.

In vipassanā one develops right understanding of one's daily life. I heard someone say that in vipassanā he is tearing himself away from normal life. He calls his life without awareness his normal life and his life with awareness his "meditation life". If we separate mindfulness from our daily life and consider it as something apart from it we are not on the eightfold Path.

For many of us it is difficult to see that the eightfold Path is the development of understanding of our daily life. The eightfold Path is the "middle way". When our understanding is more developed we will realize what the middle way is. Walking the middle way means not forcing ourselves to things for which we have no accumulations. If we have no accumulations for a secluded life it is clear that such a life is not our real life, and thus we should not force ourselves to it on the assumption that paññā will develop more quickly. There is no self who could hasten the development of paññā.

Question: I still think that there are certain conditions which are not favourable to the development of mindfulness and which should be avoided. For example, reading books such as novels. If we read books which are not about Dhamma and which do not contribute to the improvement of society, the reading is not helpful for the arising of kusala cittas. Should we not stop reading books like that if we want to have more awareness?

Nina: When we read books which are not helpful for kusala it shows that we have accumulations for reading them. It would be wrong to assume that in order to be mindful we should stop reading them; this would not help us to know ourselves and it would make us believe that we have no more akusala cittas. Not our desire to control sati but right understanding of what the object of sati is can condition its arising. Whatever reality appears, no matter whether it is pleasant or unpleasant, kusala or akusala, can be the object of sati. When there is awareness of the nāma and rūpa which appear while we are reading we are on the middle way; we are on the way to know ourselves better. There can be awareness of seeing as a type of nāma; of knowing the meaning of what we read as another type of nāma. We may be absorbed in what we read and like or dislike may arise; these are different types of nāma again. Many types of nāma and rūpa may appear while we are reading. If there is mindfulness of what appears at the present moment, also while we are reading, there will be less attachment to the concept of self.

If we have accumulations for music or for painting we should not suppress them in order to have more mindfulness. While we play music or while we paint, nāma and rūpa appear through the six doors. Why can there not be mindfulness of them? In this way we will understand that our life consists of nāma and rūpa. We do not have to go to a secluded place in order to look for nāma and rūpa; they appear already.

Question: But if we read unwholesome literature or take alcoholic drinks will it not hinder awareness? I doubt whether it is the middle way to give in to these things. It seems that there are then more akusala cittas instead of less.

Nina: Akusala cittas are bound to arise but sati can be mindful of the akusala citta. At the moment of mindfulness there is kusala citta instead of akusala citta. It is sati which can prevent us from unwholesome courses of action (akusala kamma patha) through body, speech and mind. We can learn that even a moment of mindfulness, be it only a short moment, is very valuable, that it bears great fruit, because during that moment right understanding is being developed. We will have less ignorance of our defilements; we will learn that they are types of nāma which arise because of conditions.

Someone who has developed paññā to the degree that it can realize nāma and rūpa as they really are could become a sotāpanna (streamwinner) even shortly after akusala citta appeared. When insight has been highly developed it can know any reality which appears as it is, even if it is akusala. Paññā can understand whatever reality appears as impermanent, dukkha and anattā. But only one of these three characteristics can be known at a time. Wisdom is developed in daily life and enlightenment can occur in daily life.

When we have learned from our own experience that the middle way which the Buddha taught is the only way leading to the end of defilements, our confidence in his teachings will increase all the time. We should not be afraid to be mindful of realities in daily life. Then we will know ourselves more and more until finally there will be no doubt that what we used to take for self are only nāma and rūpa.

Question: Sati has to be developed in daily life. But when I think of the day which has passed and I realize how little mindfulness there has been, I cannot help regretting the time I wasted. I know regret is unwholesome, but what can I do about it?

Nina: People would like to have a great deal of sati but they do not realize for what purpose they want it. Our aim should not be just awareness, without developing understanding, but it should be: to see realities as they are. At the very moment of awareness of the reality which appears paññā can investigate its characteristic so that eventually nāma and rūpa can be known as impermanent and non-self.

If the reality of the present moment is regret there can be awareness of that characteristic and it can be understood as it is: only a type of nāma which is conditioned. You will realize that all phenomena which arise, sati included, arise because of conditions and that it is of no use to regret the lack of sati. Then there will be less regret.

Question: Must sati always experience an object? I have heard people say that when sati is more developed it does not experience an object; that there is just stillness and peace.

Nina: Sati must experience an object. Sati is a sobhana cetasika (beautiful mental factor) arising with a sobhana citta. Each citta must experience an object and the cetasikas arising with the citta experience that object as well. Sati in samatha experiences an object; it experiences the same object as the citta it accompanies, that is: a meditation subject which can condition calm. Sati in vipassanā experiences an object; it experiences the same object as the citta it accompanies, that is, a nāma or a rūpa appearing at the present moment.

Most people like to have tranquillity and peace of mind. For what purpose do they want it? Deep in their hearts they do not want to know themselves, they just want tranquillity; they cling to a concept of tranquillity. What is peace of mind or tranquillity? There should be a precise understanding of its characteristic. There is peace or calm with every kusala citta. When one is generous or one abstains from unwholesome deeds or speech there is calm. In samatha one can develop a higher degree of calm, but through samatha defilements are not eradicated. There is calm also with the kusala citta which develops vipassanā. But the aim of vipassanā is not the calm which is temporary freedom from defilements; the aim is the development of right understanding of realities. Through right understanding the wrong view of self and eventually all defilements can be eradicated. We should know the difference between the way of development and aim of samatha and of vipassanā. Vipassanā is a kind of wisdom, it is the wisdom which knows things as they are.

Question: The Buddha said that mindfulness should be cultivated at any time, even just before we fall asleep. We read in the *Satipaṭṭhāna-sutta* (Middle Length Sayings I, no. 10[1]) that the Buddha said to the monks:

> *And further, monks, a monk, in going forward and back, applies clear comprehension; in looking straight on and looking away, he applies clear comprehension; in bending and in stretching, he applies clear*

---

[1] I have used the translation of the Wheel Publication no. 19, Buddhist Publication Society, Sri Lanka.

> *comprehension; in wearing robes and carrying the bowl, he applies clear comprehension; in eating, drinking, chewing and savouring, he applies clear comprehension; in attending to the calls of nature, he applies clear comprehension; in walking, in standing, in sitting, in falling asleep, in waking, in speaking and in keeping silence, he applies clear comprehension. Thus he lives contemplating the body in the body...*

Can there be mindfulness while we are falling asleep? When we are in deep sleep and not dreaming there are bhavaṅga-cittas (life-continuum), cittas which do not experience an object impinging on one of the six doors[1]. When we are dreaming there can be kusala cittas, but mostly there are akusala cittas.

Nina: If mindfulness has been developed there can be mindfulness just before we fall asleep. If there is no sati, there may be attachment, we are pleased to be comfortably lying down. Or perhaps we are worrying about many things which have happened during the day and thus aversion, dosa, arises. If there is mindfulness of the realities which appear just before we fall asleep, there are conditions for mindfulness as soon as we wake up. When we fall asleep we do not know whether we will wake up again. Death can come at any time. If we develop right understanding of realities in daily life, no matter what we are doing, there are conditions for mindfulness shortly before death. The cittas arising shortly before death condition the rebirth-consciousness of the next life. The sutta can remind us to development mindfulness of nāma and rūpa at any moment, even just before we fall asleep.

Question: The Buddha said that there should be mindfulness when speaking and mindfulness when keeping silence. I find it very difficult to be mindful when talking to other people.

Nina: We may think that we cannot be aware in such situations when we still assume that in order to be aware we have to do something special. When you are walking, are there no realities appearing?

Question: Yes, there is for example the characteristic of hardness which may appear, or the characteristic of motion or pressure.

---

[1] Bhavanga-cittas arise in between the processes of cittas which experience an object through one of the six doors, they keep the continuity in the lifespan of a being.

Nina: When you are talking is there no hardness, no motion?

Question: Yes, there is.

Nina: Can there not be hearing, seeing and thinking too when you are talking? Do you have to stop talking in order to notice that there is sound?

Question: No, it can be noticed while one is talking.

Nina: Can there not, while you are speaking, be awareness of sound, and can it not be known as only sound, a kind of rūpa? While we are speaking there are many different realities appearing at different moments. We do not have to stop speaking in order to be aware. When we are talking in a way which is not wholesome, when we are laughing and enjoying ourselves, we may think that we cannot be aware. But all realities are nāma and rūpa. Why can there not be awareness of them?

When you are in your office, do you often use the telephone? Are you mindful when you pick up the receiver and speak?

Question: When the telephone rings and I lift up the receiver there are so many things happening one after the other. It is difficult to be mindful in the office.

Nina: Are there no realities appearing through the six doors? You cannot be mindful all the time, but if you have right understanding of what sati is and what the object of sati, it may sometimes arise, even when you are in your office. There may be mindfulness when you take up the receiver and start to speak; then you may become absorbed in what you want to say and there is forgetfulness instead of sati. But even if there are only a few moments of sati, they can condition the arising of sati again, later on. Sati can only be gradually accumulated.

Question: Some people think that when mindfulness has not yet been established it is necessary to be alone in order to cultivate it. Is that right?

Nina: When there is mindfulness of a characteristic of nāma or rūpa we are actually alone, because at that moment we are not attached to "someone" or "something". There are no people, only nāma and rūpa. Being alone in this sense has nothing to do with the place where we are. We do not have to break off our activities in order to be aware, because any reality appearing through one of the six doors can be the object of mindfulness. Even when we are with many people we can be "alone" with nāma and rūpa.

When there is mindfulness of nāma and rūpa we will see that what we take for a "person" are only nāma and rūpa. If we were to go to a secluded place in order to be aware we might not be "alone" at all, we might instead be attached.

We read in the *Kindred Sayings* (IV, Saḷāyatana-vagga, Kindred Sayings on Sense, Second Fifty, Ch II, § 63, By Migajāla):

At Sāvatthī was the occasion (for this discourse)...

Then the venerable Migajāla came to see the Exalted One... Seated at one side he thus addressed the Exalted One:

" 'Dwelling alone! Dwelling alone!' Lord, is the saying. Pray, lord, to what extent is one a dweller alone, and to what extent is one a dweller with a mate?"

"There are, Migajāla, objects cognizable by the eye, objects desirable, pleasant, delightful and dear, passion-fraught, inciting to lust. If a monk be enamoured of them, if he welcome them, if he persist in clinging to them, so enamoured, so persisting in clinging to them, there comes a lure upon him. Where there is a lure there is infatuation. Where there is infatuation there is bondage. Bound in the bondage of the lure, Migajāla, a monk is called 'dweller with a mate'...

A monk so dwelling, Migajāla, though he frequent jungle glades, hermitages and lodgings in the forest, remote from sound, remote from uproar, free from the breath of crowds, where one lodges far from human kind, places suitable for solitude–yet is he called 'dweller with a mate.'

Why so? Craving is the mate he has not left behind. Therefore is he called 'dweller with a mate.'

But, Migajāla, there are objects cognizable by the eye, desirable, pleasant, delightful and dear, passion-fraught, inciting to lust. If a monk be not enamoured of them... the lure fades away. Where there is no lure, there is no infatuation. Where there is no infatuation, there is no bondage. Freed from the bondage of the lure, Migajāla, a monk is called 'dweller alone'...

Thus dwelling, Migajāla, a monk, though he dwell amid a village crowded with monks and nuns, with laymen and women layfollowers, with rājahs and royal ministers, with sectarians and their followers–yet is he called 'dweller alone'. Why so? Craving is the mate he has left behind. Therefore is he called 'dweller alone'."

Chapter 17

Right Concentration

Questioner: Right concentration, sammā-samādhi, is one of the factors of the eightfold Path. There is concentration in samatha and there is concentration in vipassanā. What is concentration in vipassanā?

Nina: Samādhi is a cetasika, mental factor, which is one-pointedness or concentration, ekaggatā cetasika. Each citta can experience only one object and the function of ekaggatā cetasika, which is also called samādhi, is to focus on that one object.

Each citta is accompanied by ekaggatā cetasika or samādhi, but since there are many kinds of citta there are also many kinds of samādhi. When samādhi accompanies akusala citta it is also akusala and when it accompanies kusala citta it is also kusala.

There is sammā-samādhi or right concentration in samatha. It focuses on one object: on the meditation subject which conditions calm. There are many degrees of right concentration in samatha. As calm develops and higher stages of calm are attained, concentration also develops.

There is sammā-samādhi in vipassanā. The sammā-samādhi of the eightfold Path arises together with sammā-diṭṭhi, right understanding, and sammā-sati, right mindfulness. Its object is the reality which appears through one of the six doors.

Question: Thus, sammā-samādhi focuses on the nāma or rūpa which is the object of mindfulness. It seems that we have to concentrate for some time on nāma or rūpa; but in that way there could not be mindfulness during our daily activities.

Nina: One-pointedness on the nāma or rūpa which appears does not mean concentration for a period of time. Sammā-samādhi of the eightfold Path arises with right mindfulness and right understanding which investigates a characteristic of nāma or rūpa. It arises and falls away together with the citta it accompanies. In vipassanā one does not try to concentrate for some time on the reality which appears.

The development of vipassanā does not interfere with our daily activities; whatever nāma or rūpa appears in our daily life can be object of mindfulness. Is there no seeing now, or hearing now? They can be object of mindfulness. When we are talking to other people, there are nāma and rūpa appearing through the six doors. Why can there not be mindfulness of them? We do not have to stop talking when there is mindfulness of a nāma or rūpa which appears. Sati can be a condition to speak with kusala cittas instead of akusala cittas.

Question: What should I do to understand the nāma or rūpa which appears at the present moment? There is mindfulness in my daily life, but there is not yet clear understanding of the nāmas and rūpas which appear. It seems to me that there can be mindfulness also without knowing characteristics of nāma and rūpa. Is that right?

Nina: When we begin with the development of the eightfold Path there is not yet a clear understanding of the nāma or rūpa which is the object of mindfulness. Moreover, there are many degrees of understanding. The understanding is bound to be very vague in the beginning, but, if there is mindfulness of nāma and rūpa more often, there will be a more precise understanding of their characteristics.

In vipassanā you do not have to do anything special in order to develop right understanding of the reality which appears, such as trying to concentrate on it. When there are conditions for right mindfulness it arises, and at that moment right understanding can investigate the characteristic of the reality which appears; and there is also right concentration which focuses on that reality. We should not forget, however, that right understanding cannot be developed within a short time, and thus a great deal of patience is needed for its development.

Question: Some people say that in order to develop vipassanā there must be the development of samatha as a foundation. They think that when concentration is developed in samatha it can help with the development of insight.

Nina: Samatha is the development of calm which is temporary freedom from defilements. There are sati and paññā also in samatha but these are different from sati and paññā in vipassanā and they have a different object. The way of development of samatha is different from the way of development of vipassanā and they each have a different aim. In samatha the object of sati and paññā is a meditation subject which can condition calm; in samatha one does not learn to see the nāmas and rūpas which appear as they are and thus detachment from the concept of self cannot be realized.

People may be inclined to think that they should develop samatha before they develop vipassanā in order to accumulate a great deal of sati, but they should remember that sati in samatha is different from sati in vipassanā. The aim of the development of vipassanā should be from the beginning *understanding*, understanding realities as they are, as impermanent, dukkha and non-self. This can only be achieved through mindfulness of the nāma or rūpa which appears now, at this moment.

Question: In the case of nervous people would it not be better to develop at least some degree of samatha before they develop vipassanā?

Nina: If one has accumulations for samatha one can develop it, but through samatha one does not learn to be mindful of the nāmas and rūpas which appear now, one at a time, in order to know them as non-self. How could samatha then be a necessary condition for vipassanā?

There are no rules as to the types of kusala someone should develop, because this depends on his accumulations. If nervous people were to study the Buddha's teachings and practise what he taught, they would gain more understanding of the phenomena of their lives. This understanding would help them effectively.

Question: I have heard people say that someone who is restless should not study the Buddha's teachings because it would make him more confused. He should just practise, not study.

Nina: Everyone is confused before he listens to the teaching of the Dhamma and studies it. We all have ignorance; because of ignorance we are still in the cycle of birth and death. We have eyes, ears, nose, tongue, bodysense and mind; we have lobha, attachment, dosa, aversion, and moha, ignorance, arising on account of what we experience through the senses and through the mind-door. But so long as we are ignorant we do not know about these realities.

However, in studying the teachings and pondering over them

we begin to have more understanding of our life. Could a clearer understanding make us confused? Moreoever, how could one practise without study? If we were to develop vipassanā without studying we would not know what the right path is and what the wrong path. When people do not know the characteristic of sammā-sati of the eightfold Path, they would mistakenly think that sati can be induced, they would not know that sati is anattā, non-self. The result would be that they become more attached to the idea of self, instead of less attached. They may believe that they can exert control over realities, that they can experience nāma and rūpa as they are, that they can experience their arising and falling away, whereas in reality they do not know anything. We should remember that studying the teachings is a necessary condition for the development of the eightfold Path.

Question: But should those who are just beginning to develop mindfulness not go to a special place such as a meditation centre where there is peace and quiet? Most people are so busy in their daily lives that it is impossible for them to be aware. In a meditation centre they can really set their mind on being aware and they can concentrate on nāma and rūpa.

Nina: The idea of going to a meditation centre in order to set one's mind on being aware is motivated by the wrong view of self who can control realities. A centre can be useful if one receives instruction in the Dhamma, but one should not believe that one must go to a centre in order to have more mindfulness. In the centre there may be attachment to tranquillity and this is akusala, thus not helpful. One may become more and more attached to tranquillity. When calm is disturbed there are conditions for dosa. When people return to daily life they find that they cannot be mindful, because daily life is not tranquil. Some people think that they are "in meditation" while they are in the centre and that they are "out of meditation" when they are leading their ordinary, daily life.

In the development of vipassanā there is no question of "in meditation" or "out of meditation". There are nāma and rūpa no matter where we are. Seeing now is not different from seeing in a meditation centre; seeing is always seeing, it experiences visible object everywhere. Hardness which appears now is not different from hardness in a meditation centre; it is a kind of rūpa which can be experienced through the bodysense. Right understanding of mindfulness of the eightfold Path is the condition for its arising in any place, at any time.

Question: I have heard people say that someone who begins to develop vipassanā should be slow in all his movements, he should also eat and walk slowly, in order to have more mindfulness.

Nina: When you move your arm slowly in order to have more mindfulness, what types of citta motivate the movement? Is there desire?

Question: Yes, there is desire for sati.

Nina: Thus there are cittas rooted in attachment, lobha-mūla-cittas. At such moments one thinks of the awareness one wishes to have, of what has not appeared yet. One is clinging to what may arise in the future instead of attending to the present moment. One may be ignorant and forgetful of the desire which has arisen and when seeing or hearing appears there is no mindfulness of them either. Thus there will not be detachment from the concept of self.

When one eats slowly in order to have more sati there is again clinging to sati instead of right mindfulness. When we are eating, defilements are bound to arise since we have not eradicated them. There can be like or dislike of the food we are eating, but there can be mindfulness of like and dislike so that they can be known as conditioned nāmas. No matter whether we are doing things quickly or slowly, realities are appearing through the six doors and sati can perform its function of being mindful of them. Also when we are walking quickly hardness, for example, may appear and it can be object of mindfulness.

We should not forget the second noble Truth: craving is the origin of dukkha. So long as there is clinging to nāma and rūpa there will be rebirth and thus no end to dukkha. When we in the development of vipassanā cling to results, we forget the second noble Truth. For instance, we may want to know within a short time the difference between nāma and rūpa, such as the difference between seeing and visible object, hearing and sound; or we may wish to experience the arising and falling away of nāma and rūpa. But so long as we cling to obtaining the results of the development of insight, there is no way to come to know the truth. The eightfold Path cannot be developed within a short time. In order to become detached from the concept of self a precise understanding of the different nāmas and rūpas which appear has to be developed.

Question: When there is more mindfulness there is more peacefulness too. I am inclined to be contented with peacefulness and not to develop a keener knowledge of realities.

Nina: When there is mindfulness one is at that moment removed from akusala and thus there is peace. There is also calm in the development of vipassanā. There are many degrees of calm or peace. When one has become an arahat one is freed from defilements forever. Then one has attained true peace.

One may be attached to calm which arises when there is sati. This kind of attachment is a reality which can also be known when it appears: it is only a type of nāma. We can see how deeply rooted defilements are: if there is lack of sati one regrets the lack of sati, but when sati arises one is attached to it. Awareness of all kinds of realities is essential in order to become detached from the concept of self. If one is glad that mindfulness arises one should not think that one has reached the goal. Right understanding is the aim and thus one should persevere in the development of a keener knowledge of the characteristics of nāma and rūpa.

Question: In the *Satipaṭṭhāna-sutta* (Middle Length Sayings I, 10), it appears that meditation subjects of samatha are also included in the four Applications of Mindfulness. For example, meditation subjects such as mindfulness of breath, meditations on corpses and on the repulsiveness of the body are included in "Mindfulness of the Body". Why are the objects of samatha and of vipassanā not separated? I thought that we should not confuse these two ways of mental development.

Nina: Samatha and vipassanā are different ways of mental development and they each have a different aim, as we have seen. When one reads the scriptures one will come across texts on the development of right concentration which has reached the stage of absorption, jhāna. This does not imply that all people should develop calm to the degree of jhāna. We read in the scriptures about monks who led a secluded life, developed jhāna and later on attained enlightenment. They developed jhāna because they had accumulated the skill and the inclinations to do so. Before the Buddha's enlightenment and his teaching of Dhamma, samatha was the highest way of kusala. However, those who developed jhāna and then attained enlightenment could not have attained it without having developed vipassanā as well. Some people in the Buddha's time developed both jhāna and vipassanā and then attained enlightenment, but there were also many people who developed vipassanā and attained enlightenment without having developed a high degree of calm first. The Buddha did not set any rules with regard to samatha as a necessary preparation for the development of vipassanā. The Buddha encouraged those who could develop calm to the degree of jhāna to be mindful of realities in order to see also jhāna as non-self. However, we should remember that the attainment of jhāna is extremely difficult and that only very few people can attain it. Someone who has accumulated the skill and inclination to develop samatha to the degree of jhāna, has to know the right conditions for jhāna and he has to know which factors can obstruct it. He has to be aware of his cittas in order to know whether the jhāna-factors have been developed to the degree that jhāna can be attained. If he is not attached to jhāna he can, after the jhānacittas have fallen away, develop right understanding of whatever reality appears. Also jhānacitta can be object of mindfulness, it can be realized as non-self. Anything which is real and which appears can be object of mindfulness.

Out of his great compassion the Buddha spoke about everything which is real. He knew the different accumulations of people and thus he used many different ways of explaining the truth and he taught all kinds of wholesomeness. It depends on someone's accumulations which type of kusala citta arises at a particular moment: there may be kusala cittas which ponder over the true nature of realities, or kusala cittas with a higher degree of calm, even to the degree of jhāna, or there may be kusala cittas with mindfulness of nāma and rūpa, or even lokuttara cittas which experience nibbāna.

Mindfulness of breathing and other objects which are among the meditation subjects of samatha are included in the "Application of Mindfulness of the Body", because they can also be objects of mindfulness in vipassanā. In the *Satipaṭṭhāna-sutta,* after the section on mindfulness of breathing, the section on the repulsiveness of the body, the section on meditations on corpses and after each of the other sections, we read that one should contemplate the origination-factors and the dissolution-factors in the body. In order to understand the meaning of this sutta we should not overlook these sentences. The contemplation of the origination and dissolution of phenomena is not merely thinking about them, it is contemplation through insight. The aim of the four Applications of Mindfulness is not calm which is only temporary but the wisdom which can eradicate defilements. This wisdom, insight, can only be developed through mindfulness of whatever reality appears now.

All the objects included in the four Applications of Mindfulness can remind us of the true nature of reality, of impermanence, dukkha and anattā. They can exhort us to be mindful of what appears now. The meditations on corpses can for some people condition calm, and for those who have accumulated skill for jhāna, even calm to the degree of jhāna, it all depends on the individual. However, in order to eradicate defilements, also the person who has attained jhāna should develop insight; he should with insight contemplate the origination and dissolution of realities[1]. The person who develops both jhāna and insight and the person who develops insight alone should be aware of whatever reality appears in order to eradicate wrong view and all defilements. We read in the *Satipaṭṭhāna-sutta,* at the end of each of the meditations on corpses, that the monk should reflect as follows: "Verily, this body of mine too is of the same nature as that body, is going to be like that body, and has not got past the condition of becoming like that body." Also for those who have no inclination to develop jhāna subjects such as meditations on corpses can be objects of mindfulness in vipassanā: when they see a dead person or a dead animal, they can be reminded of the impermanence of their own body. At such a moment mindfulness of whatever reality appears can arise. We may not have accumulations to reflect on corpses, but we can still think of the shortness of life and this can help us to have less attachment and aversion and not to waste opportunities for the development of right understanding of nāma and rūpa.

There are many moments of forgetfulness of realities but we can be reminded of the true nature of realities by the things we

[1] For such a person jhāna is then the "proximate cause" for insight (Vis. XI, 121).

perceive in our daily life. The "Repulsiveness of the Body", for example, which is classified under Mindfulness of the Body, can remind us to be aware. In our daily life we can notice "parts of the body", such as hair, nails, teeth and skin. Is it not true that they are loathsome? Are they not subject to decay? They can remind us of the true nature of phenomena. When we reflect on the truth there may be moments of calm, but are we contented to have only the calm which is temporary freedom from akusala? If our aim is the development of right understanding and if we do not cling to calm there can be mindfulness of whatever reality appears. Everything in our life can urge us to be mindful of the nāma or rūpa which appears now. When we look into a mirror and notice that we are becoming older it can remind us of the true nature of the body. What we take for "my body" are only elements which are impermanent and not self. Are there not many things in our life which are ugly or unpleasant, such as, for example, our own or others' bad breath? Repulsiveness and decay both in ourselves and in others can lead us to the most useful thing in life: to the development of right understanding of realities.

The Buddha spoke about everything which is real, because the objects which can remind us to be aware of the present moment are different for each of us, as we all have different accumulations. It depends on the accumulated conditions what type of citta arises at a particular moment. It may be a citta with calm reflecting on impermanence, a citta with calm to the degree of jhāna, experiencing a meditation subject with absorption, or a citta with mindfulness of the present reality. We cannot force ourselves to have a particular citta, then we are led by clinging to the concept of self. Thus, there is no rule which kind of kusala should be developed at a particular moment. Insight can be developed of the realities which naturally arise in our life.

Everything within us and around us can remind us to be aware now. Reflections on our own accumulations can lead us to awareness of the present moment too. We may notice how deeply rooted clinging is; we have accumulated it in countless lives. Do we wish to continue accumulating clinging or do we want to walk the way leading to the end of clinging? Even our akusala cittas can remind us to be aware of the present moment.

Sometimes we may notice that others have akusala cittas; we

may notice their attachment, anxiety, ignorance and doubt. Or we may notice that they have kusala cittas with generosity and compassion. The cittas of others are also included in the four Applications of Mindfulness, in the section on mindfulness of citta. They can remind us of reality and thus they can be the condition for the arising of sati. Sati can then be aware of whatever nāma or rūpa appears.

There is not any reality which is excluded from the Applications of Mindfulness. We do not have to do complicated things in order to develop the eightfold Path. That which is closest to ourselves, the realities within ourselves and around ourselves in daily life, can be the object of mindfulness at any time. Anything in the world can urge us to develop the eightfold Path, until the goal is reached: the eradication of lobha, dosa and moha.

We read in the *Kindred Sayings* (V, Mahā-vagga, Book I, Kindred Sayings on the Way, Ch II, § 9) that in Pāṭaliputta the venerable Bhadda came to see Ānanda and said to him:

> *" 'The righteous life, the righteous life!' is the saying, friend Ānanda. Pray, friend, what is the righteous life, and in what does it end?"*
>
> *"Well said, well said, friend Bhadda... Well, friend, it is just that ariyan eightfold way, namely: Right understanding, right thinking, right speech, right action, right livelihood, right effort, right mindfulness and right concentration. The destruction of lust, the destruction of hatred, the destruction of illusion, friend,— that is what this righteous life ends in."*

Chapter 18

The Highest Blessings

In the *Mahā-Maṅgala-sutta* (The Highest Blessings, Sutta-Nipāta II, 4, vs. 258–270, Khuddaka Nikāya)[1] we read that a deva came to see the Buddha when he was staying at Anāthapiṇḍika's monastery at the Jeta Grove, and asked him what the highest blessing was. In reply the Buddha spoke to him about the highest blessings. All the blessings of a life full of Dhamma are to be found in this sutta. We read that the Buddha said:

Not to associate with fools, to associate with the wise, and to honour those who are worthy of honour–this is the Highest Blessing.

To reside in a suitable locality, to have done meritorious actions in the past, and to set oneself in the right course–this is the Highest Blessing.

Vast learning, (skill in) handicraft, a highly trained discipline, and pleasant speech–this is the Highest Blessing.

Supporting one's mother and father, cherishing wife and children, and peaceful occupations–this is the Highest Blessing.

Liberality, righteous conduct, the helping of relatives, and blameless actions–this is the Highest Blessing.

To cease and abstain from evil, abstention from intoxicating drinks, and diligence in virtue–this is the Highest Blessing.

Reverence, humility, contentment, gratitude and the opportune hearing of the Dhamma–this is the Highest Blessing.

Patience, obedience, seeing the Samanas (holy men), and (taking part in) religious discussions at proper times–this is the Highest Blessing.

Self-control, Holy Life, perception of the Noble Truths, and the realisation of Nibbāna–this is the Highest Blessing.

If a man's mind is sorrowless, stainless, and secure, and does not shake when touched by worldly vicissitudes–this is the Highest Blessing.

Those who thus acting are everywhere unconquered, attain happiness everywhere–to them these are the Highest Blessings.

---

[1] I am using the translation by Walpola Rahula, in "What the Buddha taught". The P.T.S. translation is by K.R. Norman.

"Not to associate with fools, to associate with the wise, and to honour those who are worthy of honour" is the first blessing. The last blessing, which is the blessing of the arahat, cannot be attained if one lacks the first blessing. If one does not know the right conditions for enlightenment, nibbāna cannot be realized. We read in the *Kindred Sayings* (V, Mahā-vagga, Book XI, Kindred Sayings on Streamwinning, Ch I, § 5) that the Buddha asked Sāriputta to tell him what the conditions are for "stream-winning", the attainment of the first stage of enlightenment. We read that Sāriputta answered:

> *"Lord, association with the upright is a limb of stream-winning. Hearing the good Dhamma is a limb of stream-winning. Applying the mind is a limb of stream-winning. Conforming to the Dhamma is a limb of stream-winning."*

Conforming to the Dhamma is applying the Dhamma, practising it. We cannot hear the Dhamma, investigate the truth of it and practise it, unless we have met the right person who can point out to us the meaning of the Buddha's teachings and the way to practise them.

Do we want to associate with foolish people or with wise people? It is of no use to apply ourselves to mental development if we do not scrutinize ourselves first with regard to this question. We are inclined to associate with people who have the same ideas and who like or dislike the same things as we ourselves. In the *Kindred Sayings* (II, Nidāna-vagga, Ch XIV, Kindred Sayings on Elements, § 14) it is said that "through an element" beings come together. In the teachings realities are sometimes called "elements" (dhātu). An element is an ultimate reality which has its own characteristic. Elements are devoid of self. Our accumulated inclinations are like elements; the same elements attract each other. We read:

> *Through an element it is, monks, that beings flow together, meet together. Beings of low tastes flow together, meet together with them of low tastes. They of virtuous tastes flow together, meet together with them of virtuous tastes. So have they done in the past. So will they do in the future. So do they now in the present.*

When we are together with someone for a long time we cannot help being influenced by him. If we have foolish friends who do not know the value of kusala, who act and speak in an unwholesome way, it is to our decline. We may not notice that we are under their influence, but gradually we may find ourselves following their ways. If we have friends who know the value of kusala, who are generous, perform good deeds and speak in a wholesome way, it encourages us to more wholesomeness. The Buddha pointed out the dangers of wrong friendship and the benefit of righteous friendship.

Fools do not know what is wholesome and what is unwholesome. They praise what should not be praised and do not honour to those who should be honoured. For example, high esteem is given to the most beautiful woman in the country or the world, or to persons who have the greatest skill in the field of sports, or to the best actor or musician. Should we disapprove of people who have beauty, strength or skill? We cannot force ourselves not to admire them, but if we have right understanding of kusala and akusala, we will know whether it is wholesome or unwholesome to be attached to beauty, strength and skill. We will know whether these things lead to the welfare of ourselves and others or not.

How confused is life if one is ignorant of the Dhamma. One does not know what is wholesome and what is unwholesome; one does not know about cause and effect in life. When one suffers one does not understand why this has to happen. In everyone's life there is at different times the experience of pleasant objects and the experience of unpleasant objects through the senses; there is the experience of the vicissitudes of life. We read in the *Gradual Sayings* (Book of the Eights, Ch I, § 5, Worldly Failings) about the "worldly conditions" (lokadhamma):

> *Monks, these eight worldly conditions obsess the world; the world revolves around these eight worldly conditions. What eight?*
>
> *Gain and loss, fame and obscurity, blame and praise, contentment and pain...*

How susceptible we are to those worldly conditions. We are so sensitive to the way people treat us. We attach great importance to blame and praise, to honour and dishonour. If we do not receive the honour we think is due to us we feel slighted. We have feelings of bitterness towards those who treat us badly. If we do not make the career in life we were hoping for, or if work is assigned to us which we consider to be beneath our dignity, we feel frustrated. There are many things in life which cause us to feel irritated, depressed or angry. Is there one day when everything goes according to our wishes, one day of perfect happiness? When we do not have right understanding we are obsessed by the "worldly conditions"; we are foolish people.

The Buddha pointed out the dangers of being enslaved to these worldly conditions. To what does such enslavement lead? It leads to an unhappy rebirth. Devadatta, who caused a schism in the order and who separated from it with five hundred monks, was a fool; he was obsessed by the worldly conditions and corrupted by evil friendship. We read in the *Gradual Sayings* (Book of the Eights, Ch I, § 7, Devadatta) that the Buddha, while he was staying on Vulture's Peak, not long after the departure of Devadatta, said to the monks:

> *... Monks, mastered by eight wrong states, Devadatta, with his mind out of control, became one doomed to suffer in hell, in perdition, dwelling there a kappa*[1]*, irreprievable. By what eight?*
>
> *Mastered by gain... by loss... by fame... by obscurity... by honour... by lack of honour... by evil intentions... by evil friendship, with his mind out of control, Devadatta became one doomed to suffer in hell, in perdition, dwelling there a kappa, irreprievable....*

Fools like Devadatta who are obsessed by worldly conditions cannot teach Dhamma. They want others to follow them blindly. They do not lead people to the Buddha's teachings so that they can investigate the truth for themselves. If we associate with fools we cannot develop right understanding of our life. We will become more obsessed by the worldly conditions and there will be no way for us to eradicate defilements.

The Buddha, "Teacher of devas and men", taught out of compassion for the world, not in order to have "gain, honour and praise" in return. He pointed out that it is the Dhamma which is

[1] A "world-period" or aeon, an inconceivably long space of time.

important, not the person who teaches it. We read in the *Kindred Sayings* (III, Khanda-vagga, Kindred Sayings on Elements, Middle Fifty, Ch IV, § 87, Vakkali) that the Buddha visited Vakkali who was sick and who was so attached to the sight of the Buddha. Vakkali said:

> *"For a long time, lord, I have been longing to set eyes on the Exalted one, but I had not strength enough in this body to come to see the Exalted One."*
>
> *"Hush, Vakkali! What is there in seeing this vile body of mine? He who sees the Dhamma, Vakkali, he sees me; he who sees me, Vakkali, he sees the Dhamma. Verily, seeing the Dhamma, Vakkali, one sees me; seeing me, one sees the Dhamma.*
>
> *As to this, what do you think, Vakkali? Is body permanent or impermanent?"*
>
> *"Impermanent, lord."*
>
> *"Is feeling... perception, the activities, is consciousness permanent or impermanent?"*
>
> *" Impermanent, lord."*
>
> *"Wherefore, Vakkali, he who thus sees... he knows '... for life in these conditions there is no hereafter'. "*

Further on in this sutta we read that Vakkali took the knife in order to kill himself. The Buddha told the monks that Vakkali had attained arahatship before he died. He could become an arahat because he had developed insight to that degree.

The wise person does not want others to follow him blindly, but he helps them in such a way that they can realize the truth themselves, without being dependent on him; this is the most effective way one can help others. He leads them directly to the Buddha's teachings and encourages them to study the "Tipiṭaka", the three Collections of the Vinaya, the Suttanta and the Abhidhamma. Then they can have wise consideration of the teachings and verify the Dhamma themselves. He points out the way by which they can realize for themselves the truth of impermanence, dukkha and anattā. The aim of the Buddha's teachings is to see realities as they are. So long as we have not realized the truth we take for permanent what is impermanent, we take for happiness what is not happiness, we take for self what is non-self.

We read in the *Kindred Sayings* (IV, Saḷāyatana-vagga, Kindred Sayings on Sense, First Fifty, Ch III, § 26, Comprehension) that the Buddha said:

> *Without fully knowing, without comprehending the all, monks, without detaching himself from, without abandoning the all, a man is incapable of extinguishing dukkha.*
>
> *Without fully knowing, without comprehending, without detaching himself from, without abandoning what (all) is a man incapable of extinguishing dukkha?*
>
> *It is by not fully knowing the eye... objects... eye-consciousness... eye-contact... that pleasant or unpleasant or indifferent feeling... the tongue... savours... the body... touches... the mind... mind-objects...*[1] *that a man is incapable of extinguishing dukkha. This is the all, monks, without fully knowing which... a man is so incapable.*
>
> *But by fully knowing, by comprehending, by detaching himself from, by abandoning the all, one is capable of extinguishing dukkha.*

The Buddha pointed out the impermanence of seeing, hearing and all the other realities which can be experienced through the six doors, in order to remind people to be aware of the seeing at this moment, of the hearing at this moment. If we are not mindful of seeing-consciousness which appears at the present moment or of the other realities appearing now, there will not be a precise understanding of their characteristics and thus we will not be able to see them as they are. The wise person does not teach a Dhamma which is different from the Buddha's teachings. He does not point out things which do not lead to the goal. He does not discourage people from study and he does not discourage them from being mindful during their daily activities. He encourages them to be mindful of the reality appearing at the present moment, no matter where they are and what they are doing. It is essential to find out whether the person with whom we associate is the right friend in Dhamma or not. If he is not the right person he cannot point out to us the way to see things as they are. We will know that he is the right person if he helps us to understand the

[1] Also the ear, sound, the nose, odour, the contacts through the ear, the nose and the other doorways, and the feelings arising conditioned by those contacts are included in the "all", as is explained in § 23, "The all".

characteristic of seeing which appears now, of hearing which appears now, and of the other realities which present themselves through the six doors. This is the way the Buddha taught as the one and only way to eradicate the clinging to the concept of self, to see things as they are. When there will be less attachment to the concept of self we will know from our own experience that association with the wise is the highest blessing.

To honour those who are worthy of honour is the highest blessing. The Buddha, the Dhamma and the Sangha are worthy of honour. The wise person who taught us the development of the eightfold Path is worthy of honour. How can we honour those who are worthy of honour in the most appropriate way? We feel deep gratitude to the Buddha and we want to give expression to our gratitude. We can honour him by following his last words: "Transient are all the elements of being! Strive with earnestness!" (Mahā-Parinibbāna-sutta, Dialogues of the Buddha II, no. 16). We should not be heedless, we should be mindful of realities. Without the Buddha's teachings we could not be mindful at this moment and there would be no way to eradicate defilements. The whole purpose of the teachings is the eradication of defilements through the development of right understanding. Therefore, each moment of mindfulness is the highest possible way of respect to the Buddha, the Dhamma and the Sangha.

"To reside in a suitable location" is among the highest blessings. We cannot meet the good friend in Dhamma in just any place; wise people are rare in the world. It is a great blessing to live in a country where Dhamma is taught and practised, so that one has an opportunity to know the Buddha's teaching. There are many factors that have to coincide in order to meet the right person. It is not by mere chance that we meet him; it is conditioned by kamma, by good deeds which have been performed.

When someone meets a wise person he may not be ready yet to receive the Dhamma. It may not be the right time for him to listen to the Dhamma; he may not be capable yet of wise consideration of the teachings. The accumulation of wholesome deeds is very helpful for making us ready to receive the Dhamma. "To have done meritorious actions in the past" is among the highest blessings. We read in the "Thera-therīgāthā" that the men and women in the Buddha's time who attained enlightenment had accumulated meritorious deeds for aeons and that they had also listened to the Dhamma preached by Buddhas of former times. We read, for example, about Subhā (Commentary to the Therīgāthā, the Paramattha-Dīpanī, commentary to Canto XII, 70, Subhā):

> *She, too, having made her resolve under former Buddhas, and accumulating good of age-enduring efficacy, so that she had progressively planted the root of good and accumulated the conditions for emancipation, was, in this Buddha era reborn at Rājagaha...*

Subhā listened to the Buddha, developed insight and attained enlightenment, even to the stage of the arahat. When we know about the conditions necessary for wisdom to reach maturity we will be less inclined to think that it is self who develops the eightfold Path. When we read that men and women in the Buddha's time had accumulated good of "age-enduring efficacy", that they had listened to the Dhamma preached by former Buddhas, before they met the Buddha Gotama and attained enlightenment, we are reminded not to be heedless at the present time.

The Buddha taught satipaṭṭhāna to monks, nuns, laymen and women layfollowers. As regards the life of the monk, the Vinaya should not be separated from satipaṭṭhāna. In the Buddha's time the Vinaya and satipaṭṭhāna were not separated. We read in the "Mahā-Maṅgala-sutta that one of the highest blessings is "a highly trained discipline" (vinaya). The commentary to this sutta (the Paramatthajotika) speaks about the discipline of the layman, abstinence from the ten immoral actions[1], and about the discipline of the monk. The monk who develops the eightfold Path will have a deeper understanding of the Vinaya and he will observe the rules more perfectly. Each detail of the Vinaya is full of meaning because the rules support the welfare of the community of the monks, the Sangha, and help the monk to lead a pure life; the rules help him to be considerate in his speech and actions, to cause no trouble to others. The Vinaya teaches the monk to be watchful in body, speech and mind. When we develop mindfulness

[1] These are three unwholesome actions through the body, which are killing, stealing and sexual misbehaviour. There are four unwholesome actions through speech, which are lying, slandering, rude speech and idle speech. There are three unwholesome mental actions, which are covetousness, ill-will and wrong views.

there is watchfulness as regards the six doors. Through right understanding of nāma and rūpa we will come to know our subtle defilements and the danger of even these defilements. The monk who develops satipaṭṭhāna will have a deeper respect for the rules of the Vinaya which remind him to be watchful, seeing danger in even the slightest faults. Thus we see that Vinaya and satipaṭṭhāna should not be separated.

The monk who develops the eightfold Path and attains enlightenment will not leave the order anymore and return to the "lower life", the layman's life. We read in the *Kindred Sayings* (V, Mahāvagga, Book I, Ch VI, § 12, The river) that the Buddha spoke by way of simile about the monk who will not return to the layman's life; he said that the river Ganges, tending towards the east, cannot be made to change its course and tend towards the west. We read:

> *Just so monks, if the rājah's royal ministers or his friends or boon companions or kinsmen or blood relatives were to come to a monk who is cultivating and making much of the ariyan eightfold way, and were to seek to entice him with wealth, saying: "Come, good man! Why should these yellow robes torment you? Why parade about with shaven crown and bowl? Come! Return to the lower life and enjoy possessions and do deeds of merit"— for that monk so cultivating and making much of the ariyan way, return to the lower life is impossible. Why so? Because, monks, that monk's heart has for many a long day been bent on detachment, inclined to detachment, turned towards detachment, so that there is no possibility for him to return to the lower life...*

The eightfold Path can change the lives of monks and laypeople. It can change the relationship between parents and children, husband and wife, relatives and friends. There is bound to be attachment and displeasure or anger in one's relationship with others, but when satipaṭṭhāna is developed there will be less clinging to the concept of self and this will bear also on our relationship with others. When other people treat us badly we can remember that in the ultimate sense there is no self or person who suffers, and that there is no person who behaves in a disagreeable way. There are only nāma and rūpa arising because of conditions.

We are still susceptible to the worldly conditions of gain and loss, honour and dishonour, blame and praise, well-being and pain. It is unavoidable that there are both pleasant and unpleasant experiences in our life: one day there is blame, the next day there is praise. However, when we learn that receiving blame or praise are only phenomena which arise because of conditions and fall away immediately, we will gradually attach less importance to them. We read in the Mahā-Maṅgala-sutta:

> *"If a man's mind is sorrowless, stainless, and secure, and does not shake when touched by worldly vicissitudes–this is the Highest Blessing."*

Those who are arahats have a mind unruffled by worldly conditions, they are free from sorrow, free from defilements. Nothing can disturb the arahat any more. The sutta continues:

> *"Those who are thus acting are everywhere unconquered, attain happiness everywhere–to them these are the Highest Blessings."*

We are not free from sorrow. So long as there is clinging to the concept of self there is no end to lobha, dosa and moha. Our defilements are the real cause of the suffering in our life, day after day. The Mahā-Maṅgala-sutta tells us about the blessings of a life full of Dhamma. We read about lovingkindness in the relationship between parents and children, between husband and wife, between relatives and friends. We read about righteous conduct, diligence in virtue, reverence, humility, patience, self-restraint, a holy and pure life. When we read about all these blessings we may feel at times discouraged about the practice of the Dhamma. We are inclined to think that the eightfold Path is too difficult and that we are too far from the realization of the truth. We would like to have less lobha, dosa and moha; but can we force ourselves not to be attached to pleasant things, not to be disturbed by unpleasant things? We should always remember that the Buddha became enlightened and taught the truth for our welfare and happiness. The Buddha taught the Dhamma which can be practised in daily life. "To set oneself in the right course" is among the highest blessings. When we have associated with a wise person who can explain the Dhamma to us, when we have listened to the Dhamma and carefully considered it, we can set ourselves in the right course. Defilements cannot be eradicated immediately, but if there is less ignorance of realities we can experience that it is a blessing to have been able to listen to the Dhamma. Through the development of satipatthāna the notion of self will gradually decrease until it is finally eradicated. And, thus, we will experience the highest blessings of the Dhamma.

Glossary

abhidhamma, the higher teachings of Buddhism.

adosa , non aversion.

akusala, unwholesome, unskilful.

alobha, non attachment, generosity.

amoha, wisdom or understanding.

anāgāmī, non returner, person who has reached the third stage of enlightenment, he has no aversion (dosa).

Ānanda, the chief attendant of the Buddha.

anattā, not self.

anicca, impermanence.

appanā, absorption.

arahat, noble person who has attained the fourth and last stage of enlightenment.

ariyan, noble person who has attained enlightenment.

arūpa-brahma plane, plane of existence attained as a result of arūpa-jhāna. There are no sense impressions, no rūpa experienced in this realm.

arūpa-jhāna, immaterial absorption.

āsavas, influxes or intoxicants, group of defilements .

bhāvanā, mental development, comprising the development of calm and the development of insight.

bhavanga-citta, life-continuum.

bhikkhu, monk.

bhikkhunī, nun.

bodhisatta, a being destined to become a Buddha.

Brahma, heavenly being born in the Brahma world, as a result of the attainment of jhāna.

brahma-vihāras, the four divine abidings, meditation subjects which are: loving kindness, compassion, sympathetic joy, equanimity.

Buddha, a fully enlightened person who has discovered the truth all by himself, without the aid of a teacher.

Buddhaghosa, commentator on the Tipiṭaka, author of the Visuddhimagga in 5 A.D.

cetanā, volition or intention.

cetasika, mental factor arising with consciousness.

citta, consciousness, the reality which knows or cognizes an object.

dāna, generosity, giving.

deva, heavenly being.

Devadatta, the Buddha's cousin. He tried to kill the Buddha as well as causing a schism in the order.

dhamma, reality, truth, the teachings.

Dhammasangaṇi, the first book of the Abhidhamma Piṭaka.

Dhātukathā, Discussion on the Elements, the third book of the Abhidhamma.

diṭṭhi, wrong view, distorted view of realities.

dosa, aversion or ill will.

dukkha, suffering, unsatisfactoriness of conditioned realities.

ekaggatā, concentration, one-pointedness, a cetasika which has the function to focus on one object.

hetu, root, which conditions citta to be "beautiful" or unwholesome.

jhāna factors, cetasikas which have to be cultivated for the attainment of jhāna: vitakka, vicāra, pīti, sukha, samādhi.

jhāna, absorption which can be attained through the development of calm.

kāmāvacara cittas, cittas of the sense sphere.

kamma patha, course of action performed through body, speech or mind which can be wholesome or unwholesome.

kamma, intention or volition; deed motivated by volition.

kappa, an endlessly long period of time.

karuṇā, compassion.

khandhas, aggregates of conditioned realities classified as five groups: physical phenomena, feelings, perception or remembrance, activities or formations (cetasikas other than feeling or perception), consciousness.

kilesa, defilements.

kusala citta, wholesome consciousness.

kusala kamma, a good deed.

kusala, wholesome, skilful.

lobha, attachment, greed.

lokiya citta, citta which is mundane, not experiencing nibbāna.

lokuttara citta, supramundane citta which experiences nibbāna.

magga, path (eightfold Path).

mettā, loving kindness.

Moggallāna, The second of the Chief disciples of the Buddha

moha, ignorance.

muditā, sympathetic joy.

nāma, mental phenomena, including those which are conditioned and also the unconditioned nāma which is nibbāna.

ñāṇa, wisdom, insight.

nibbāna, unconditioned reality, the reality which does not arise and fall away. The destruction of lust, hatred and delusion. The deathless. The end of suffering.

Pacceka Buddha, silent Buddha, an enlightened one who has found the truth by himself but does not proclaim Dhamma to the world.

paṭisandhi citta, rebirth consciousness.

Pāli, the language of the Buddhist teachings.

paññā, wisdom or understanding.

paramattha dhamma, truth in the absolute sense: mental and physical phenomena, each with their own characteristic.

parinibbāna, "complete Nibbāna"–complete extinction of Khandha Life. i.e. all possibility of such life and its rebirth.

rūpa, physical phenomena, realities which do not experience anything.

rūpa-brahma plane or rūpa-bhūmi, fine material realm of existence attained as a result of rūpa-jhāna.

rūpa-jhāna, fine material absorption, developed with a meditation subject which is still dependant on materiality.

sakadāgāmī, once-returner, a noble person who has attained the second stage of enlightenment.

samādhi, concentration or one-pointedness, ekaggatā cetasika.

samatha, the development of calm.

sammā, right.

Sammā-Sambuddha, a universal Buddha, a fully enlightened person who has discovered the truth all by himself, without the aid of a teacher and who can proclaim the Truth to others beings.

Sangha, community of monks and nuns. As one of the triple Gems it means the community of those people who have attained enlightenment.

Sāriputta, The first chief disciple of the Buddha.

sati, mindfulness or awareness: non-forgetfulness of what is wholesome, or non-forgetfulness of realities which appear.

satipaṭṭhāna sutta, Middle Length Sayings 1, number 10, also Dīgha Nikāya, dialogues 11, no. 22; .

satipaṭṭhāna, four applications of mindfulness: Body, Feeling Citta, Dhamma.

sīla, morality in action or speech, virtue.

sobhana (citta and cetasika), beautiful, accompanied by beautiful roots.

sotāpanna, person who has attained the first stage of enlightenment, and who has eradicated wrong view of realities.

sutta, part of the scriptures containing dialogues at different places on different occasions.

suttanta, a sutta text.

Tathāgata, literally "thus gone", epithet of the Buddha.

Theravāda Buddhism, 'Doctrine of the Elders', the oldest tradition of Buddhism.

Tipiṭaka, the teachings of the Buddha.

upacāra, access or proximatory consciousness, the second javana-citta in the process in which absorption or enlightenment is attained

upekkhā, indifferent feeling. It can stand for evenmindedness or equanimity and then it is not feeling.

vācī, speech.

Vinaya, Book of Discipline for the monks.

vipākacitta, citta which is the result of a wholesome deed (kusala kamma) or an unwholesome deed (akusala kamma). It can arise as rebirth-consciousness, or during life as the experience of pleasant or unpleasant objects through the senses, such as seeing, hearing, etc.

vipassanā, wisdom which sees realities as they are.

viriya, energy.

Visuddhimagga, an Encyclopaedia of the Buddha's teachings, written by Buddhaghosa in the fifth century A.D.

vitakka, applied thinking.

With bad advisors forever left behind,
From paths of evil he departs for eternity,
Soon to see the Buddha of Limitless Light
And perfect Samantabhadra's Supreme Vows.

The supreme and endless blessings
of Samantabhadra's deeds,
I now universally transfer.
May every living being, drowning and adrift,
Soon return to the Pure Land of
Limitless Light!

~The Vows of Samantabhadra~

I vow that when my life approaches its end,
All obstructions will be swept away;
I will see Amitabha Buddha,
And be born in His Western Pure Land of
Ultimate Bliss and Peace.

When reborn in the Western Pure Land,
I will perfect and completely fulfill
Without exception these Great Vows,
To delight and benefit all beings.

~The Vows of Samantabhadra
Avatamsaka Sutra~

DEDICATION OF MERIT

May the merit and virtue
accrued from this work
adorn Amitabha Buddha's Pure Land,
repay the four great kindnesses above,
and relieve the suffering of
those on the three paths below.

May those who see or hear of these efforts
generate Bodhi-mind,
spend their lives devoted to the Buddha Dharma,
and finally be reborn together in
the Land of Ultimate Bliss.
Homage to Amita Buddha!

NAMO AMITABHA

南無阿彌陀佛

財團法人佛陀教育基金會 印贈
台北市杭州南路一段五十五號十一樓

Printed and donated for free distribution by

The Corporate Body of the Buddha Educational Foundation

11F., 55 Hang Chow South Road Sec 1, Taipei, Taiwan, R.O.C.
Tel: 886-2-23951198 , Fax: 886-2-23913415
Email: overseas@budaedu.org
Website:http://www.budaedu.org

Printed in Taiwan
15,000 copies; November 2005
EN196-5433